FLETCHER WASHINGTON

A Generational View on Wealth

(An Autobiography)

Life is not a race or competition where only one person wins and everyone else loses. It is more of a lifelong journey where everyone has the opportunity to enjoy both wins and loses along the way regardless of their 'starting line'. All you have to do is continue moving forward and plant seeds along the way – and you will reap what you sow.

Fletcher Washington: A Generational View on Wealth

Written by Fletcher Washington

ISBN: 978-1-7357204-3-2 (paperback)

10 9 8 7 6 5 4 3 2 1

First Edition: February 2023

TABLE OF CONTENTS

INTRODUCTION 10

PART I – THE STARTING LINE 15

EARLY CHILDHOOD (1970-1978) 18

CONFLICT OF INTEREST (1988-1992) 22

PART II – MOVIN' ON UP 34

ASCENDING ABROAD (1993-1996) 54

JUMPING SHIP (2002-2007) 61

PROMOTION PROTOCOL (2017-2022) 74

PART III – SHOW ME THE MONEY 101

WHEELS UP (1979-1988) 104

FINANCIAL ADVANTAGE (1988-1992) 107

THE BRASS TAX (1992-2022) 109

THE INFLECTION POINT (2022) 120

CHANGE OF PLANS (2022-Now) 128

I WISH (Now) 147

PART IV – THE HANDOFF 161

FAMILY MATTERS (Now) 163

WONDER WOMAN (1993-2017) 166

LIKE FATHER, LIKE SON (2002-Now) 171

CONCLUSION 180

APPENDIX 183

PREVIOUS MILITARY ASSIGNMENTS 183

MY BROTHERS & SISTERS 207

ADDITIONAL PICTURES 212

SMALL QUIRKS ABOUT ME 214

A TRIBUTE TO MY MOM

I honestly believe that anyone who knew my mom was glad to see her finally taken from this Earth because she was one of the more deserving people to have a place in Heaven. Her 68 years were long, tiring, and fulfilling because she endured tragedy upon tragedy her entire life but continued to persevere after each blow. I find comfort in the fact that she was saved and believed in God, and He never makes a mistake. I know deep down she is exactly where she has always wanted to be.

To put it lightly, my mother was dealt a bad hand in life. She was born on August 5, 1933 and endured 68 long years. Losing her mother at age three, her father raised her and her siblings in a small four-room house he built with his hands with no running water. They only ate what was grown in the garden. She left home around the age of 21, to marry my father, who was initially hard-working, but later became an alcoholic and spouse abuser.

Neither she nor my father went past the ninth grade, although it was common during that time and in their socio-economic environment to simply quit school and raise a family. Over time she developed diabetes causing numerous health problems including poor blood circulation in a leg that ultimately had to be amputated. I am convinced that there were more complications with diabetes that sent her to her home in heaven.

Regardless of the hardships she faced (and please know what I've shared only scratches the surface), she persevered by putting her faith and love in God and her children. Through her children, she accomplished great achievements that are ordinarily unimaginable from someone of her financial, educational, social, and economic background. All eight children graduated from high school. None of her children have ever been incarcerated. Five out of eight kids joined the military. Three children have Master's degrees. Nearly all eight children are either happily married, own their own home, and/or work respectable jobs. All of this may not sound exciting to you, but when put in perspective of just how far we've come out of the projects filled with prostitution and drugs, these achievements are remarkable and a direct reflection and result of our mother. Funny enough, my mother could have cared less about college or even the Master's degrees. She was far prouder to see us graduate from high school.

I am sure anyone reading this can tell an equally impressive story about their own parents. If they are still around, I challenge you to tell them just how appreciative you are every chance you can get. As for me, I will continue to use every opportunity I get to show how my mom, against all odds, managed to turn her lemons into lemonade for the sake of her children.

Thank you, Mom, for loving me unconditionally through all your hardships and setting a good example for following a spiritual path in the midst of your many storms.

Love Always,

Fletcher

INTRODUCTION

How do you attain true happiness *and* success? It only took 40 years, but I believe I figured out the answer to this Million Dollar question. Growing up wasn't easy. You name any social service hand-out, and I guarantee my family received it: welfare, food stamps, Section-8 housing… by depending so heavily on government assistance, we had everything but happiness and success. I can attest that when you want something so bad, you will do whatever it takes to make it happen. Often it takes finally achieving what we were after in the first place to realize that we had it all wrong to start with.

By the age of 43, my investments surpassed the one-million-dollar mark. Many would say that is unquestionably a form of success in the financial sense. I was promoted to a one-star Brigadier General in the Army at the age of 46. Even more would say that was as a matter of fact a form of success in the professional sense. But it was not until I attained both that I realized neither were the answers to *real* happiness. Now that I am older and wiser, I realize that I am most happy whenever I do *great* things. I am talking about those things that don't necessarily benefit or bring attention to me, but honorable things that are selfless, charitable, and result in putting a smile on someone's face. I am talking about giving more than I receive whether it be money, respect, or mentorship. I am talking about keeping a positive energy around my superiors *and* subordinates. I am talking about making everyone I have the chance to interact with feel wanted and needed. What is the point of success if you have no one to share it with? After all these years in search of happiness, I've come to realize that it is homemade.

This applies to any facet of life you want to consider. *Real* happiness, in my opinion, is based on the return on investments (ROI) you receive from the way you live your life and the way you treat others. I always hated hearing the very cliché saying of "money can't buy happiness." Each time I would hear that over-used line, I would only think under my breath, "Sure, money may not buy happiness, but it can certainly buy *things* that might make you happy!" I would dream about a luxury car for me, diamonds for my lady, expensive vacations, chocolate, or whatever else your vice might be at any given time. But now I can say with 100% certainty that those *materialistic* things are superficial and here today but gone tomorrow. That return-on-investment (ROI) however you can gain from helping someone less fortunate or taking a younger individual under your wing in mentorship or someone you mentor is something you can't place a price tag on. That kind of happiness is strong enough to stick with you. We have all heard the popular saying, "life is what you make it." The question is do you truly believe you can make the life you have always dreamed of?

I am often told by many how they are so proud of me for accomplishing all that I have, especially considering my *starting line* in life was pushed back a little farther than most. I have reached great heights thus far in life and still have energy in my body to stride even farther. In this autobiography, I will relay why many of my brothers, sisters, and I have such a burning desire to run as far and as fast as we can away from our *starting line.* It would be selfish and arrogant to think that I achieved all my success alone. Much of my success is a result of the kindness, mentoring, and respect that I received from others over the years. I've made it a point to "pay it forward" to others and in turn, my blessings have been returned ten-fold. I am a firm believer in God and give Him all the glory for my many successes. As Philippians 4, 13 says: "*I can do all things through Christ who strengthens me.*" As I reflect on my life, I am often reminded of the popular hymn that reads (original lyrics by Curtis Burrell):

"I Don't Feel No Ways Tired, I've Come Too Far From Where I Started From.
Nobody Told Me That The Road Would Be Easy.
I Don't Believe He Brought Me This Far To Leave Me."

This is not a self-help book, and I don't intend for you to feel bad for me as you start to understand where I come from. I am simply telling my story from my vantage point. If anything, take this book as a survival guide for the hardships that you may face. Consider this a blueprint for where you hope to go. Let this be an indicator that the challenges you face today will all be worth it in the end as long as you maintain a glass half full approach to life. View obstacles as opportunities to grow, regardless of how big or small they may be. You will be amazed just how much more resilient you become over time. Things don't get easier as you move on and move up, you just learn to handle situations better than before. I hope that you enjoy my 'rags to riches' story and if you pay close enough attention, you will discover a roadmap on how you can do the same.

Hopefully, this autobiography will make you want to be the type of person who gives more than you take often, generally enjoys putting a smile on the faces of those less fortunate than yourself, and brings life to an inspirational quote. Mark Linton, a fraternity brother and author, once wrote "A real man is the kind of man that when your feet hit the floor each morning the devil says, 'Oh Crap, he's up!'" Never underestimate the power that you wield to make a difference *even* with your own happiness. See you at the end.

PART I – THE STARTING LINE

The concert hall was in pristine condition as friends and family started to assemble in. The floors seemed like they had never been walked on. The sheen alone might as well have struck a conversation with you. Norfolk State pulled out all the stops by renting out this venue and it seemed like it was just for me. I adjusted my uniform as my ROTC peers started to move. Pomp & Circumstance played louder and louder as I briskly kept pace behind my classmates. The cadence brought me back to ROTC Summer Camp. As I sat down, I immediately found my family in the stands. They didn't seem surprised at all. After all we had been through, this was just another day for them. Someone came to the podium to speak, but my mind started to wander. "I finally made it." As I sat waiting for my name to be called, I started to reminisce on just how far I had come.

This was my most pivotal moment. Although that answer may be commonplace for a question of that degree, my reasons are different. Sure, other siblings graduated and moved on, but they weren't me. They didn't do what I did. I call this particular moment out not because of what the degree has done for me or the new status I immediately received within the military. It is because my starting line was no longer behind everyone else's. Let me explain. God has gifted each and every one of us an opportunity to live, but what isn't up for decision are the families that we are born into and the foundation already built just for us. For me, there was no foundation and there were hardly any tools to even prepare such a thing for my family, let alone my legacy. My starting line as I like to call it required me to go farther, overcome obstacles, and avoid pitfalls that others just didn't have to. Needless to say, I walked across that stage upon graduating regardless of where I came from or what I had been through. I finally could breathe a sigh of relief knowing that I no longer had to play catch up. Little did I know, my starting line has always been right where it needed to be to get me to where I am today.

Life was never fair. But in that moment, I realized that would never limit me again.

EARLY CHILDHOOD (1970-1978)

I was born August 28, 1970 in Fredericksburg, Virginia. I have an extremely large family consisting of five older sisters and two older brothers. My father was one of 13. And although my mother was only one of three, her father was one of 11 so as you can imagine, I have cousins and cousins, and even more cousins. If you thought my family was big then, you should look at them now.

My mother was (in her earlier years) one of the strongest women I knew. It may not have been physically, but she could go toe to toe with anyone socially and mentally. She overcame numerous hardships in her life including but not limited to segregation, poverty, the loss of her mother at age three, and raising all eight of her children virtually by herself. Although my parents were married while having all eight of their children, my father was not an ideal parent. He was an alcoholic and a wife beater. My parents, who only completed the ninth grade, were married at a time when education was not as important. It was common to simply quit school to take care of younger family members or to marry early and raise a family of your own. I remember just how difficult things were for me and my siblings because of the amount of money flowing in the house. To help you with the answer, what's 1 + 2 - 3? My father, who worked every day, chose to spend his money elsewhere and prioritized everything else over us. Oftentimes he didn't even come home after work. I recall a few days where we went the entire day without food and even more days than I care to remember where the meal of the day was buttered bread and sugar water. We may not have rounded out all our food groups, but it was enough to survive.

We did not have running water in the house in the rural county of Stafford, which I lived in up until age nine. Oftentimes the well would run low and since we never had the money to have it repaired, we had to walk great distances to neighbors' homes to first borrow and then tote the water back home in buckets. Moreover, Stafford was more rural during my childhood, which meant the distance that we carried these bucket-loads of water was a minimum of a quarter mile or more. Keep in mind that we could not borrow from the same person each time. So, when we went beyond the next-door neighbor to three, four, or five houses beyond ours, the distance was a mile or more where we toted these bucket-loads of water. Is it truly borrowing if we never returned any water? Every time a friend came over to visit, we would hope he or she did not have to use the restroom because it was very embarrassing to say we did not have one. Our restroom consisted of an empty living-room coat-closet. In place of a typical closet door there was a bed sheet nailed across the entrance way of the small coat-closet and in place of a typical toilet there was the 'dreaded bucket.' We simply used a plastic pail kept in a closet with no door, dumped the bucket in the woods behind the house, and then washed and replaced the bucket back in the closet after each use.

If you have ever seen poor people before in your life, you could lift that rock bottom up to find us. I always told myself that I built character in those early days. One Christmas, I remember taking the pedals off my bicycle a week prior, wrapping them up in a brown grocery bag and placing them under my bed. It made me appreciate every moment to use them. I would replace those pedals temporarily with a pair of vice-grip pliers. It was so inconvenient and uncomfortable. Then on the big day after opening my only present and putting the pedals back on, I felt as though I had gotten a new bicycle. You'll see later why this was such a big deal. Even now that money is the least of my concerns, I still doubt that I will ever be able to top that awesome gift I gave myself years ago.

Obviously, I would not wish a childhood like that on anyone. I would not wish a father who acted like mine on anyone either. But, I am a positive person and believe there are small nuggets of worth and teaching points in every situation. We only need to have the strength and courage to see beyond our present circumstance to see the bigger picture. There is a popular saying that says something like *"Do not be afraid of going outside your comfort zone and stretching into areas that are new and uncomfortable, because that is where growth lies."* Regarding my father's parenting, or lack thereof, and the positive that came out of that, Steve Harvey (the popular comedian) tells a story about how you can learn from everyone and how he even learned from his father even though he didn't have the best intentions for him. Just like Steve, I learned what *not* to do from my father. Although that was meant to be a joke, there is a lot of truth to the notion that you can learn just as much from a bad example as a good one. Just like those pedals, as an example, is a gift nonetheless. It's all about what you do with it.

One of my older brothers spent a night in jail for shooting our father in the leg with a shotgun for beating on our mother. He was only a juvenile still in High School and no charges were filed but our father did carry a well-deserved limp, for the remaining 15 years he lived, to his grave. To break from this impoverished lifestyle, my older sisters and brothers either enlisted in the military or married after graduation from high school. This was a means to get out of the house and our impoverished lifestyle as soon as possible.

CONFLICT OF INTEREST (1988-1992)

On February 27, 1988, I enlisted in the Army National Guard. I was only in my senior year of high school and 17 at the time when I signed the papers, but I knew that I wanted to leave my neighborhood, go off to college and make something of myself. The National Guard offered the best opportunity to do just that. Even though I had to get my mother to sign special forms giving me permission to join, I was surer than ever of my decision. The two primary reasons I enlisted in the National Guard were money and money. I was so fixated on the money that I might have been blinded and biased with no thanks to my recruiter who walked me through the process. That's right. I too was tricked by my recruiter like so many other young enlistees then and now. After I told my recruiter my primary objective was money for college, he showed me all the MOSs that had the highest sign-up bonuses.

My military occupational specialty (MOS) was 12-Bravo, Combat Engineer. The National Guard was a great vehicle of opportunity for me. Here's the rub: the more tactical the MOS (think Infantry, Armor, Artillery, etc.), the shorter the life expectancy during combat. Because of this, they had higher signing bonuses. Any young gun looking for a quick buck would jump at the chance to risk their life. A Combat Engineer MOS had a very high bonus. Mind you, $2,000 was considered high at that particular time although they are as much as $30,000 nowadays. I told my recruiter that I was going to college so I could eventually become a manager somewhere down the road in my civilian life, so I was not interested in having an MOS as a Grunt or anything similar where I had to play in the field all day. He told me that the Combat Engineer MOS would be perfect for me. He explained how I would wear a hard hat and learn engineering and I would also receive the bonus which would be very helpful for college. I did end up receiving the bonus, but instead of a hard hat, I was issued a steel pot (kevlar helmet) and all the rest of the equipment that a standard Infantryman receives. I quickly learned in basic training (and later at my actual unit) that a 12-B Combat Engineer is the closest thing to an 11-B Infantryman – I should have guessed that from the MOS numbers alone as they are too close for comfort. I guess I was blinded by the dollar signs. I didn't hurt too bad as I honestly needed the biggest bonus I could get to help out with college.

I was assigned to the 229th Combat Engineer Battalion of the 29th Light Infantry Division. In layman's terms, I was a grunt. This particular division was known as a 'Sapper' unit which focused on training young individuals such as me to go to the field with only what we could carry on our backs. We were to Combat Engineers as Rangers are to Infantrymen. As part of the course, we would stay out in the field for days and sleep out in the elements. Picture rain, snow, and hail all greeting us and only a poncho to show for it. Tents for whatever odd reason were nowhere to be found, something a commander would probably get relieved of command for forcing their soldiers to do in today's Army. It is almost comical how the Army has softened up year over year. Regardless, I still have the fondest memories of frostbite every time my hands and feet get cold. As common with frostbite, and the lessor form known as chilblains, it causes long-term nerve damage. Because of this, my hands and feet freeze up much easier than most people.

The Army runs two Sapper schools: one for the Active Component at Fort Leonard Wood, Missouri and one for the Reserve Component at Fort A.P. Hill, Virginia. As a National Guardsman, I was attending the course at Fort A.P. Hill which is structured around a series of weekend Drills for 24 months and two summer annual training events. Fortunately for me, I never did complete Sapper school. I was in my third year of ROTC in college and had to attend my ROTC summer Advanced Camp, a mandatory ROTC event in the process of becoming an officer. Therefore, I was unable to complete the Sapper course because of missing the final two-week annual training session. Someone told me back then it was because of time constraints. I'd like to think it was the grace of God.

In June of 1988, I graduated from high school, completed basic training that summer, and began attending college that fall. Time had a mind of its own as everything moved so quickly. In the span of a few days after graduating from high school, I was on a plane flying off to Missouri to attend basic training. And within approximately a week of graduating from basic training, I was sitting in my first college class as a freshman at Norfolk State University as an enlisted soldier.

How did I get into college, you ask? I am inclined to believe that my extracurricular activities in high school had something to do with it. I was a member of Future Business Leaders of America (FBLA) and the Spanish Club. I played football, baseball, and soccer if they didn't interfere with my working schedule which meant I played only at the little league level, as I began working as a pre-teen. I even managed to obtain a yellow belt in Taekwondo. But my favorite involvement by far had to be Distributive Education Clubs of America (or DECA for short). It was everything I had come to love up to that point. It wasn't just a class that talked about money. It was a class that talked about how to *make* money. Next thing you know, I was a junior officer my sophomore year, a vice president my junior year, and president my senior year. But it was more than that. I made sure to lead by example! I was permitted to leave school early every day after lunch during both my Junior and Senior years *to go to work.* In other words, I got *paid* to go to school at a young age! That was my first exposure to what an internship actually was and I loved every minute of it.

I can also tell you how I *didn't* get into college. If I told you how low I scored on the SAT, you may stop reading this right now. No one ever told me the importance of taking the exam more than once or even preparing for the one exam I took. I wonder if things would have been different if my guidance counselors spent quality time coaching me through it all. Back then and even nowadays, good grades alone don't cut it. With that said, it was slim pickings in finding a college that 1. admitted me regardless of the scores that I received and 2. provided some form of financial aid. Lord knows I couldn't afford to cover tuition, let alone my family. So, I measured schools based on how much they were willing to pay me, I ranked every single four-year accredited university in the state of Virginia, by cost, from most expensive to least expensive, to come to the consensus that in-state was my only reasonable option. After narrowing my list drastically, to the two least expensive (Norfolk State and Virginia State, at that time in 1988), it all came down to the physical location. I thought of the sexy appeal of Hampton Roads and Virginia Beach, and was sold. As I sat at my desk listening to my first lectures, I knew Norfolk State was the perfect fit for me.

I continued drilling with my unit one weekend a month and two weeks during the summer in an enlisted capacity for four years. Fast forward a few years and I went on to graduate Cum Laude from Norfolk State earning a BA in Political Science and Economics concentrating in Public Administration with a 3.3 GPA. This was in addition to my then Cadet status and Specialist E-4 rank as part of the National Guard and completed Advanced Individual Training as part of ROTC through the split-option program. This consisted of monthly drilling for all four years. I would be remised if I didn't highlight in addition the 30 hours per week I worked as a security guard while in college.

Aside from attaining the distinctions and honors of graduating, I was a Distinguished Military Graduate from the ROTC program and scored high at Summer Camp. Summer

Camp (also known as Advanced Camp) is a six-week training exercise that Army ROTC cadets attend the summer between their junior and senior year of college. You are placed in various leadership positions and rated on several items including leadership, physical fitness, and land navigation among a few other traits and qualities a good officer should possess. Most prior-service soldiers (i.e., someone who has served in the military before) do very well in both their college ROTC classes and Summer Camp because they have already completed basic training and served as a *real soldier*. I do not mean to take anything away from the college ROTC program but for lack of better words, it is fair to say that there is no substitution for the *real thing* a soldier receives from serving in the Army as opposed to what a brand-new college student receives by attending an ROTC college class a few hours a week. A college student who enrolls in ROTC but has already completed basic training, advanced individual training (AIT) and has served in a real Army unit has a distinctive advantage. They will be one step ahead of the average college student who enrolls in ROTC but has never worn the uniform and has never served in the Army. Therefore, most cadets who are prior service, like myself, do very well in both ROTC and at Summer Camp.

During your senior year of college, you are allowed to complete a dream sheet composed of your top 10 preferences, for military branch assignment and geographic location assignment, after graduation. For most, it remains just a dream. Your performance in ROTC, rating during Summer Camp, and overall cumulative college GPA are the sole criteria to determine your choice of assignment and duty location. For some, it didn't matter what you actually selected whether you were awarded Regular Army (RA), active duty, or a Reserve commission during my college days. During my ROTC years, an RA commission was only awarded to approximately the top 20% of each graduating class. The next 30% received an active duty commission and the remaining 50% received a Reserve commission (meaning you were not accepted as an officer on active duty and were instead ordered to serve as an officer in the Army Reserve or Army National Guard). I am not completely aware of every distinction between a Regular Army (RA) officer commission and an active duty officer commission. Both commissions mean that you are full-time on Active Duty. However, RA carries somewhat of a *tenured* status. All active duty officers are automatically converted to RA status once they make Major.

But prior to making Major, there are several boards that active duty officers compete in (that RA officers did not) to be allowed to continue in the service on active duty status. Because of my high college GPA, top scores in ROTC class, and top scores during Summer Camp, I was fortunate to receive my first Branch choice of Transportation, my first duty location choice of Germany, as well as the distinguished Regular Army (RA) tenured status.

The lesson of it all: The SAT (like so many things) is prejudicial. You can't tell me that there isn't a direct correlation between SAT scores and family education, family income, and residence in cities or suburbs. I think back to who my guidance counselors were *actually* helping back in high school. I am sure they spent most of their time mentoring the kids who *looked* the part. The strategy for scoring high on the SAT and for successful college admission begins very early in a child's life. It involves intellectual stimulation from the cradle through preschool and through grade school, which most African-Americans in the lower socio-economic percentiles do not receive. For example, parents should encourage their child's ambitions by promoting reading at an early age, scheduling vacations around their child's interests to stretch their imaginations and make them think more broadly and deeply. However, vacations to old battlefield sites, museums, and scenic attraction sites in different countries (or even in different states) are the last things on the minds of a family living in the projects on welfare who do not know whether they will have electricity the next week.

In its own beauty, my performance on the SAT was my wake-up call. It was my incentive to exceed expectations and prove to myself that I am just as academically inclined (if not more) than the next person. The important thing in this scenario, as in every other thing in life, is to simply understand where you are in life and being completely honest with yourself. Don't be afraid to roll up your sleeves to put in the extra work required to overcome and/or work around your shortfalls to *still* succeed *despite* the challenges you face. The excuses that you can have are endless on what all is holding you back, but don't go for them. I went on to graduate from both Florida Tech earning a Master's degree in logistics management with a 3.9 GPA and the National Defense University earning a Master's degree in strategic studies. I thank my shortcomings every day for lighting a fire under me and reminding me that it is all just part of the process.

2nd Lieutenant First Duty Assignment in Germany

PART II – MOVIN' ON UP

On October 4, 1992, I married Rhonda Renee Price of Roanoke, VA. A graduate of both Old Dominion University (with a Bachelor's degree in Education) and the University of Maryland (with a Master's degree in Business Administration), I was way out of her league. Scratch that, I was playing a completely different game. But somehow, God gave me one of the best gifts. Just one month after marrying the love of my life, I completed my Transportation Officer Basic Course at Fort Eustis, VA. What did that mean exactly? Rhonda and I were relocated to our first duty assignment in Mannheim, Germany where I served as a Platoon Leader and Company Executive Officer. In the matter of a month, our lives were uprooted and transplanted to a foreign land, and it was there where we contended for the Guinness World's longest honeymoon. All jokes aside, we were bound to change for better or worse.

Rhonda and I did not enjoy Germany as much as we thought we would during the first year. We missed the luxury of shopping malls, convenience stores, and everything in between. To compensate for what was lacking, we did a lot of traveling during our first year in Germany. We visited France (three times), Holland (twice), Italy, Spain, Austria, England, Belgium, Iceland, and of course all over Germany. Who would have thought that getting out of our comfort zone would be our new safe place? It was during this time that I realized if change is inevitable, I might as well have a say so in just how much I grow. I have been movin' on up ever since and haven't even thought to look back.

I wore the rank of Second Lieutenant for exactly two years and was promoted to First Lieutenant in May 1994. I was a First Lieutenant again for two years and was promoted to Captain in June 1996. The rank of Captain is one of the longest ranks that you hold in the military. Generally, one would hold this rank for approximately six to seven years. I was promoted to Major while still in the Regular Army in

2003, just 10 years and 9 months after being commissioned as a Second Lieutenant. Fun fact: the promotion list was released in August 2002, but because I was commissioned in the month of May (the month a majority of Officers are commissioned because of college graduations), my sequence number was approximately in the middle of the pack. My Primary Zone consideration for promotion to Lieutenant Colonel (LTC) would have normally been the Fall of 2008. I maintained outstanding Officer Evaluation Reports and an excellent assignment history with great jobs that I have worked in the past. Because of this exceptional file, I was selected for a Below-the-Zone (BZ) promotion to LTC on 21 December 2007. Only 8% of the Officers were selected for a BZ promotion to LTC on that board. I was selected for Colonel (full bird eagle) on a 2012 promotion board and pinned the rank on 1 August 2013. I was again blessed to be selected early for Brigadier General on a 2015 promotion board and pinned the rank (a star) on 23 February 2017.

Our Wedding

Rhonda and I in Venice

One morning, when I was nine and after my mother could take no more of the abuse, she packed two medium sized plastic trash bags of our clothes and belongings, waited until our father had left for work, and moved us from the rural county of Stafford to the city of Fredericksburg. This would be my first major change and well out of my control. Just 20 minutes away from everything we knew, we were the latest recipients of governmental aid. In those early years of my life, I welcomed the social service system because Section-Eight virtually provided a rent-free and comfortable place to live (at least compared to what we had 'escaped' from in our previous situation) and the Food Stamps provided full course meals on a daily basis. Both were priceless. It's crazy to think how your perspective shifts the more you have as a reference. At the time, I only had the impoverished conditions in Stafford County to compare it to. 'Comfortable' is a relative term; relative to the person telling the story and relative to the person receiving the story. I've learned that what is 'comfortable' to one may be the complete opposite to another.

One of the things I hated most about going to visit family in Fredericksburg after I was a fully grown and successful Army officer was having old neighborhood friends run up to my car to sell me something. I saw it all from drugs to car parts to jewelry, all in an attempt to woo me. All they saw was the Mercedes pull up and immediately thought of it as an opportunity to make a quick buck. I would surprise them every time by saying, "my mother lives here." Over time, my definition of comfortable changed. The projects infested with drug dealing and prostitution were a terrible place to grow up and I am convinced that the social service system fails us (and nearly ruined me) time and time again. Hang on as we unpack that later.

After we moved to the city of Fredericksburg, our father eventually lost both his long-held jobs at the factory mill and the old run-down home in Stafford. He became homeless and somehow found his way to the city of Fredericksburg and often stayed with different friends or relatives whenever he was lucky. I often remember riding my bicycle through the city park and spotting him sleeping or drinking from his liquor bottle on a park bench. I would stop to chat with him for a few minutes every now and again. I'd even throw in a few dollars here and there. I never cared what he did with the money, but deep down it was a way to show him that the family was doing well. He died from an alcohol-related cardiac arrest when I was 14.

As the youngest of eight children, I was spoiled in many ways. You can imagine after raising all my other siblings, my mom had probably grown tired from parenting. A kid of my age should not have done some of the things I did and go unpunished for it. But just like many kids raised by an older parent or grandparent, I was allowed to get away with far more than my older siblings could. Older parents just tend to be softer on children than younger parents are. You have to remember though, by the time I came on the scene, many of my siblings no longer lived in the house. With my father long gone and two older brothers moved on, I was left to be the man of the house. I can just think of my older sisters shrugging at the thought, but how could I not take advantage of such a title? Let me be clear, I was no deadbeat. I lived a completely different lifestyle versus many of my friends around the same age. After I began working at the age of 11, as a paperboy with two (not one, but two!) dedicated paper routes, I started to contribute to the household bills. If and when anyone still in the house attempted to punish me for any wrongdoing I may have done, I would simply say, "well if you do that to me then I am not going to pay the electric bill next month." Of course, there was the occasional whipping here and there, but I am sure I deserved far more than I actually received. I could spend the night at a friend's house without asking permission and then come home the next day with no questions asked and no repercussions. That is probably the reason I had sex for the very first time at the age of nine and probably the reason one of my sisters had all four of her children by age 20.

I remember vividly my days at the local bar at age 11. Before you jump to any conclusions, there was a pool hall in the bar. One of my first stops ever when I received a paper route was to deliver a paper to this bar. I walked in to find drinking, cursing, gambling, and all the rest. But in plain sight was what looked like the best time. These pool tables were crowded, and money was on the line. I didn't know how to play pool just yet, but I knew money and there was a lot of it flying from one hand to the next. I wanted in. So, I started to study the game. I would play pool nearly every day after my shift. I made sure that stop on my route was my last.

Eventually, I ended up gambling with the grownups just for them to show me how to play at their level. They loved to play with me almost as much as I loved to play with them. They would buy beer for themselves and soda for me. In an almost odd way, the drunks cared for me as if I was their own. No one would swindle me in a game of pool, they made sure of it. Don't count me out though. I mastered the art of 'English' at a young age. For the inexperienced few who may be reading this, English refers to the control of the cue ball *after* you make impact on another ball. That's right. Based on where you hit the cue ball initially, you can control where the ball goes and ultimately set up for the next shot.

There was this one time when I finished my paper route after a long day, I walked in to find the bartender giving me a stern look. Wondering what had happened, I approached him and he handed me what seemed like a wanted sign. My picture was sprawled out across the page. I looked around and realized that everyone already knew. Earlier that day, my mother came in and gave the manager this picture of me and told them she did not ever want me to go in there again. I was to go straight home after only delivering the paper. Someone must have snitched around what was really going on. I gave a sigh and proceeded to put my head down. As I looked up, I had a soda in front of me and the bartender started to crack up. In seconds the place had busted out in laughter. I went on to play pool for money and drink my soda while they drank their beer like nothing had ever happened. I was truly too grown for my own good.

I picked up other pass times in unorthodox ways outside of pool early on. I learned to play chess from the best type of people – ex-cons. You may not know it but people in prison play a lot of chess. They have nothing much else to do so most people you meet who have served time in prison know how to play the game and play very well at that. Dominoes are also up there. I had a lot of ex-cons as friends, neighbors, and relatives who I grew up with, so I like to think I can hold my own no matter what's on the table. In my basement or game room, I have a rather nice pool table, computer, entertainment center, gym, music system, bar and two tables – one table has the chess board on it and the other table has a domino set and cards on it.

One thing that has remained constant for me in childhood and through adulthood is that I didn't have to learn to cook. Sure, I had jobs that required me to drop some chicken in a bucket of grease and set a timer. But there is a stark difference to pulling out a myriad of pots and pans, shopping for the right ingredients, and cooking something that will have to be edible not just by your standards, but those around you as well. I can't cook today because so many ladies in my life have, and continue to, cook for me. As easy as that may roll off the tongue, I can explain. Growing up, I had five older sisters and a mother cooking at home (when there was food available of course) and they all can cook very well. Within days after high school graduation, I went off to basic training, where paid government contract workers cooked for me time and time again in the military dining facility. Then, upon completion of basic training and just two days later, I was off to college where food was prepared in a cafeteria by paid employees. Next up, I got married a few months after graduating college at the young age of 22 and my wife has been cooking for me ever since.

I remember the countless times that this bit me in the butt. On two occasions, Senior Service College at the Norfolk Naval Base and Brigade Command at Fort Sam Houston, I chose to do an unaccompanied assignment without my family to keep them stabilized in one location. Other times, I would arrive to my new assignment months before the family arrived. That was me trying to be a good father and keep my son from constantly transferring schools or my wife uprooting from her job. The little skills I had for breakfast meals (cereal, oatmeal, fruit and yogurt), for lunch (sandwich and chips) only took me so far. Talk about a perfect excuse to eat out daily for dinner. I survived and lived to tell the tale. Needless to say, over the years I have gotten very comfortable cleaning. Anything used to prepare the meal doesn't stand a chance against my attention to detail. No matter pot or pan, I kept things spick and span, as I have no problem cleaning the kitchen as long as someone else does the cooking.

Was I bad? Sure. Did I press my luck? Of course. But that's the price that was paid with an awful lot of responsibility that I had that my other friends did not. I am sure glad we survived that lifestyle so we all can sit back and laugh about it now. During those early years, I would have without hesitation given up my enormous freedom of going anywhere and doing anything in exchange for a more normal lifestyle. I dreamed of living in a nice home, with clean furniture and a fully stocked fridge. It would have been nice to never have had to worry about the water being turned off or moving multiple times a year to avoid paying the rent. The list goes on. But in hindsight, I believe God had a plan all along and everything happens for a reason. There are countless examples of me accomplishing things without even knowing it. It is very likely that for me to have achieved what I have, I needed to overcome huge obstacles that the ordinary person did not. I think of the prominent presence of drugs and alcohol alone that were accessible in my neighborhood. Yet and still, I have never done drugs, never smoked a cigarette, and only rarely drink. I was so fixated at the time on getting out and making something of myself that I refused to let anyone or anything sway me otherwise. Looking back, that mindset spoke volumes of the amount of determination and discipline I had at such an early age. I was always focused on doing something, achieving something, and becoming something in life.

Having two jobs consistently throughout my pre-teen and teenage years gave me a great sense of responsibility and far more discipline than I received from going through basic training. While my school-aged friends were playing sports on the middle and high school teams, for the community on recreation leagues, or in the community on local pick-up teams in the park, I was working and paying household bills. While my peers were running through the neighborhood getting into trouble as pre-teens and teens normally do, I was acquiring a strong work ethic and lots of discipline. How could I not have hit the ground running in the right direction when I reached adulthood? I am convinced that much of my strength, humility, and will to succeed has come from such a rough childhood. Here's an example:

After my mother left our father and moved us to the city of Fredericksburg, we were able to qualify for welfare. Incidentally, she received a form of assistance her entire life even in her later years where it was in the form of disability from a leg amputation. My mother often sent me to the grocery store to buy food with food stamps since I was the only one in the house with transportation, which was only a bicycle or moped. It was extremely embarrassing to have the cashier yell into the microphone to her manager across the store to, "Please bring me change for a $50 dollar food stamp!" *Every time* an instance like that occurred, it seemed like I could *always* turn around and spot a friend from school staring at ‘that person’ (me) holding up the line and causing a most humiliating scene with food stamps.

Of course, I could go on but you can fill in any blanks you may be pondering. I don’t share this to make you re-live a terribly embarrassing memory of mine, but to simply put together just enough of the puzzle to give a good understanding of my childhood. With such humbling moments, my character was strengthened immensely to the point that it helped me to be the person I am today. The instances I mentioned above can do one of two things to you:

Scenario 1: The underprivileged childhood makes you resentful with low self-esteem. Unfortunately, you just follow the masses around you as you enter a life of drugs and crime. Money comes quick and a little too easy and your false sense of security is just as bad as it is in the welfare system. The risks have never been higher.

I saw this all too often within the four figurative walls of my neighborhood. It didn’t matter who you were. Close friends, neighbors, and relatives alike all fell into the same repetitive cycle of poverty and crime. A dependency on the welfare system starts to form and governmental assistance becomes a necessity. But let me tell you, not every opportunity is made equal. 'Milking the system' will only get you so far.

Scenario 2: The underprivileged childhood makes you yearn for a better tomorrow. You and your family have gone through so much that there is nowhere to go but up. You became strong and independent through adversities. You realize how much farther you can go in life with a little bit of humility and laughter.

Somehow, someway I split away from the crowds. I chose the path less traveled because something deep down told me I was worth more than the environment I was in. My situation gave me the sort of hunger to succeed that cannot be taught in an academic environment. As a matter of fact, the only way this is taught in my opinion is going through something yourself or following closely someone who has experienced hard times.

Here's a real-life case study for you. One of my sisters received the following from social services on a monthly basis. I've added some loose definitions for the reader that may not be privy to some struggle related terms:

a) Welfare Check: This is literally hard green cash to be used almost at your complete disposal
b) Food Stamps: Essentially cash bills but only to purchase food
c) WIC Check: A voucher accepted at most retail stores specifically given to women with infant children
d) AFDC Check: Also known as an Aid to Families with Dependent Children grant, this provides additional cash payments based on the amount of parental support
e) Section Eight: Drastically subsidized housing based on your income. For her, rent was no more than $50 per month
f) 100% College Reimbursement: Because of her income status, the government paid for all completed college courses at both the local community college and Mary Washington University

Note: These were common terms during my childhood. Some of these terms have changed, i.e., food stamps have been replaced with an Electronic Benefit Transfer (EBT) card, etc.

In addition to the governmental assistance listed above, she also worked part time and received child support (on a very irregular basis when the child's father paid). I don't say these things to ding my sister. She knows I have nothing but love for her. But I say this to showcase that the opportunity to milk the system is definitely there. Too many perks in the system can make you complacent and give no motivation to leave the system. Fortunately, the government has instituted several measures to curb this abuse and potential complacency on the system by allowing one to receive benefits for only a specified amount of time where you must show some type of progress, or you will be disenrolled from the system. You better believe there are still some loopholes in the system. I continue to see the abuse and complacency each time I visit my old neighborhood and similar neighborhoods alike.

I honestly think this same sister was the smartest of all eight of us. She could literally not study, only half-way go to school, and still make A's. I made decent grades, but I had to attend school and pay attention in class to make the grade – but not her. Unfortunately, once we moved from the country to the city, she immediately began hanging out with the wrong crowd and as they say, "the rest is history." She had all four of her kids by the time she was 20. She dropped out of high school because of the multiple pregnancies and her fast lifestyle, and raised all of her boys by herself with no help from their dads. Ordinarily, you can conclude that that type of lifestyle would involve a dependency on welfare and probably being trapped in the projects. The kids would be in and out of jail and the cycle would just continue for several generations. As a matter of fact, this was my sister's story for many years. That is until she turned over a new leaf. Although she was dependent on the social service system for a long time, she's done numerous things to better herself and has several college degrees to show for it.

She is a great example, to all who feel the odds are stacked against them, that if you have the determination and will to put in the work, that you can rise above what's weighing you down and turn your negatives into positives. In addition to no longer drinking, she is a licensed Registered Nurse (RN). Let that sink in for just a moment. Considering her *starting line* in life that she was born into, compounded by the choices she made early on by having all four of her boys early in life, and dropping out of high school, she has come an incredibly long way. For those of you who aren't familiar with nursing, there are three basic levels of nursing (there are several more levels when factoring in the 'degrees' of nursing up to a Doctorates in nursing, as well as management levels of nursing, but the three basic levels are as follows): a Certified Nursing Assistant (CNA) requires roughly a 75-hour vocational course; a Licensed Practical Nurse (LPN) requires roughly a one-year vocational course; and a Registered Nurse (RN) requires either an associate's or Bachelor's degree in nursing. Prior to completing her nursing degree, she worked as a counselor to underprivileged and abused kids while balancing night classes through and through. I never visited the camp where she worked, but I am sure she was a valuable asset as she was able to assist kids on a personal level.

She completed a Bachelor's degree from Mary Washington University in the Spring of 2007 with a four-year degree in Liberal Arts with a concentration in African American Studies. She returned to Mary Washington University a few years later to complete a Master's degree, to which she has only one remaining course to complete towards this Master's degree. She then realized she did not want to work in her initial chosen field, so she continued taking classes to earn another degree in nursing to become an RN. Along the way, she also earned a license in cosmetology, and although she allowed the license to expire after she switched to nursing, she retains the graduation diploma. And each time I talk with her, I am awestruck at the hurtles she has conquered, in relation to our *starting line* in life, as they make all my tangible (and financial) achievements pale in comparison. But all of that is something she will have to tell in her own personal autobiography. I hope she writes one because it will be far more interesting than mine. Claudia, I am proud of you and wish you all the best.

ASCENDING ABROAD (1993-1996)

During our second year overseas, we were very active in our social organizations. Time started to fly between events facilitated by these organizations as we continued to travel.

Rhonda and I in Holland (Left) and Paris (Right)

Military Ball as Lieutenant Colonel

We were in a different city every other weekend attending a litany of different meetings and social functions. Rhonda is a Life Member of the Alpha Kappa Alpha Sorority, Inc. I am a Life Member of the Alpha Phi Alpha Fraternity, Inc. and a Prince Hall affiliated Mason. Aside from being a Blue House Mason (a 3rd degree Master Mason), I also belong to the Red House (a Companion) and the Consistory (a 32nd degree Prince), and I am also a 33rd degree Sovereign Grand Inspector General (SGIG) which is the highest and last degree of masonry. It should be noted that a true Mason does not pride himself on being the highest, but rather being proficient as a 3rd degree Master Mason and living an upright and honorable life. Let me breakdown these social organizations one by one:

1.) Military

I'm not going to lie. I looked good in uniform. At a whopping 6 feet tall and weighing in at 190 pounds, it was hard not to; most tall and slim individuals look good in uniform – whether a military uniform, police uniform, etc. As an officer, I've always held key leadership positions and been responsible for millions of dollars' worth of equipment and countless soldiers and civilians. Additionally, considering my background, from humble beginnings, and having been enlisted myself, I easily maintained a healthy and respectable relationship with the soldiers and civilians under my charge.

2.) Alphas

When I consider my time so far within the lifetime membership of the Alpha Phi Alpha Fraternity Inc., I can think of three things it has meant to me: brotherhood, connection and service to the community. Believe it or not, the reason you would generally find an Alpha in Germany is because of the military, either as a service member or as a spouse of a service member, or as a government civilian assigned to a US military organization. Many were officers serving their country just like me. It was only a matter of time before incredible friendships were created with my fraternity brothers on this first assignment. What does this result in? Mentorship. I had countless senior officers at the time pour into me just by association expecting nothing in return. The feeling? Priceless.

3.) <u>Masons</u>

Masonry is the largest and oldest fraternal organization in the world. Masonry was extremely prevalent during my assignments in Germany. The brotherhood in this organization is extremely tight. For example: If I was stranded or just needed a helping hand, my Masonic brother is obligated to assist me and vice versa. However, there's a fine balance to manage when serving in the military, especially in leadership positions. Unlike my Alpha fraternity which is a college-oriented fraternity, Masonry is not. Therefore, a majority of Masonic members are enlisted members and warrant officers. You will definitely find commissioned officers as members, but not nearly as many as enlisted and warrants. So, if a Mason who is an officer with a certain level of responsibility (i.e., commander, director, chief, officer in charge, etc.) is doing special favors, receiving general assistance, or attending special and secluded social functions with a Mason who is enlisted and especially if serving under your leadership, that may be misconstrued as showing favoritism which is punishable under the Uniformed Code of Military Justice (UCMJ). Because of fraternization concerns, after my initial four-year tour in Germany, I stopped 'actively' participating with Masonic events, when holding certain key leadership positions (i.e., company commander, battalion commander, brigade commander, garrison commander, etc.) because it is not uncommon to find younger NCOs and junior soldiers as members. I will say that, as I became more senior in rank, I resumed my participation at the 33rd degree level. This is primarily because at the 33rd degree level, members are generally an older and more mature group where fraternization was much less of a concern. But now as a retiree, that is no longer a concern at all.

I was very active during my four years in Germany. After I left Germany in 1996, I have remained financially active in the other degrees because I believe in the ideals of the organization, such as the requirement to believe in God, be an upright and just man, among other noble traits. During these mid-grade years, where I was climbing through the officer ranks of the military, I only visited lodges on infrequent occasions in the various places I was assigned without holding an office where my participation was critical. I see myself even deep into my retirement years raising funds around worthy causes to help our community.

4.) AKAs

I list this because it is another organization that took up part of my time and kept me active while assigned in Germany (and still to this day), because I attended many of Rhonda's social functions with her. Who would have thought the "Divine Nine" (the nine African American fraternities and sororities, also referred to as Black Greek Letter Organizations, that make up the National Pan-Hellenic Council) would be so prevalent in Europe? Anyway, we Alphas had many joint functions with the AKAs. You see, many think the AKAs are the sister-sorority to the Alphas. There is no formal linkage between the two, but we do carry ourselves as though we are. The same can be said for the Deltas (from the esteemed Delta Sigma Theta Sorority) and the Ques (from the illustrious

Omega Psi Phi Fraternity), who also have an unofficial sister-brother relationship. However, the Zetas (from the prominent Zeta Phi Beta Sorority) and the Sigmas (from the notable Phi Beta Sigma Fraternity) do have an official sister-brother relationship among their organizations. Being surrounded by so many beautiful, young, educated ladies, and like-minded gentlemen, who all looked like me and made up the "Divine Nine," definitely helped the time go by easier while assigned and living thousands of miles away from home.

While each college campus may have different stereotypes for the different fraternities and sororities, the bottom line is that all the "Divine Nine" fraternities and sororities serve a very similar purpose and are soundly rooted with very similar tenets and principles. So regardless of which fraternity or sorority you belong to, it is all for the same cause after college is over. And even though we all joke one another about our frat/sorority being superior to another, it is just that - a joke and definitely done in jest. Deep down, we all have the utmost respect for one another because we know we, to include the Masons and Eastern Stars, are all after the same goal: to help our fellow man/woman and community through charity, service, love, mentorship and other similar traits.

JUMPING SHIP (2002-2007)

Attaining a high rank was never my goal, at least not initially during the first half of my career. My mother was far prouder to see her eight children graduate from high school than from college, so the bar has always been pretty low in my opinion. My goal was always simply to be *successful* and to make enough money to be *comfortable*. I never even saw myself completing a full career in the military, it was only a tool or means to pay for college. It's funny how the simplest decisions we make can have such drastic impacts on our lives. At the high school level, my goal in life was simply to be a 'manager' of any type of company because that is what I saw as *successful*. At least that is what it looked like from the restaurant and retail jobs I held all through middle and high school.

In order to be a 'manager,' I knew I needed a college degree. In order to attain a college degree, I needed a path or mechanism to pay for it. I chose the National Guard as that mechanism to pay for my college. Since the goal was to acquire a Bachelor's degree, in the easiest manner possible, I chose a non-STEM liberal arts major with the easiest electives I could find. Since I had already completed basic training and was already “literally” a soldier in the National Guard, I knew ROTC would be an easy elective and an ‘easy A’. Not only did I earn the ‘easy A' in ROTC, it also led to a commission in the army, whereby I became a Second Lieutenant.

After making it to the rank of Captain, and successfully completing a Company Command assignment, which is essentially the mid-point of a successful career with strong reassurance that you can make it to the 20-year mark to qualify for a retirement, the choice was easy to push on towards that “20.” However, at the mere rank of Captain (which is only two ranks beyond Second Lieutenant) my goal was still not to attain a high rank, but to simply make it to retirement at 20 years. I envisioned exiting after doing my time to an even nicer ‘manager’ level role than what I imagined in high school. This is the primary reason I switched from the Regular Army (RA) to the Active Guard/Reserve (AGR) program. Although an AGR soldier is on active duty and receives the exact same benefits as a Regular Army soldier, they are technically controlled by the Reserve Component (RC) not the Active Component (AC).

I knew that going down the AGR track was the fastest path to retirement. At least to retire with active duty by my name that is. I had already started dreaming of what that next career was going to be for me. But I didn't think this transition would happen as fast as it did or under the circumstances. In 2002 while assigned at Fort Lee, VA, I completed my first deployment and upon my return, my then Regular Army Branch Manager told me it was time to PCS with only an offer to go to Korea. There were no other options given and not a care in the world towards me or the implications it would have on my family. The choices were simply to leave the family at Fort Lee, VA while I completed a one-year unaccompanied tour to Korea (after I had *just* completed an unaccompanied deployment to Kuwait) or get out of the Army.

We have been a Nation-at-war for over two decades consistently (from 2002-2022 and beyond). It is very common to see RA soldiers who have deployed in harm's way away from their families every other year since 9-11. But back in 2002, when I completed my first deployment, when the Army had not previously deployed since the first Gulf War 10 years earlier (from 1990-1991), it was not normal to see back-to-back deployments or deployments followed by unaccompanied tours to Korea like they were recommending for me at the time. All this to say that I felt I was not being treated fairly by my Branch Manager and felt it necessary to increase my assignment options. With my son only five years old at the time, I refused to not be in his life at this critical moment for two consecutive assignments. I thought back to what a fatherless childhood creates and knew that keeping the family together was my top priority, even if it meant I had to do so without my Branch Manager's help.

I decided to submit a packet (or application in civilian terms) in hopes of first getting accepted into the AGR program to see what different Branch Managers would offer. After approximately two months since submitting, I began calling the AGR Accessions Office (the office that reviews and accepts applicants into the program) along with four different (AGR) Branch Managers. The four branches I qualified for included Transportation, Logistics, Force Management, and Branch Immaterial. I didn't discriminate and I wasn't afraid to get their attention. I called on a weekly basis to inquire what availability they had for a Major in any fields that I qualified for. Not getting the response I was looking for, I began calling twice a week. I am sure you would have done the same if your original (Regular Army) Branch Manager kept pestering and pressuring you to make a decision (between accepting the Korea assignment or getting out), neither of which were in my favor if I may remind you. Would you believe it that the AGR Logistics Branch Manager finally offered me five different options from Queens, New York all the way to Fort Buchanan, Puerto Rico. Without a second thought, Rhonda and I accepted Puerto Rico as our new home.

I made the conversion from RA to AGR without a break in service. This meant that I remained on continuous active duty without having a full day of not being in the military. The 5th of September 2003 was my last day in the RA and the 6th of September 2003 was my first day in the AGR program. I simply signed out of my last unit at Fort Lee, VA (just like any other PCS move) and the very next day my entire family flew to Puerto Rico where I immediately signed into my new unit (just like any other PCS move). There was no disruption in my pay or any other benefits, which made for a seamless and successful transition into the AGR program.

Based on my assignments since converting to AGR, most people would have never guessed that I ever converted at all. I served in the Pentagon three times, attended the War College as a 'resident' student (many Reserve officers attend the War College as a 'non-resident' student), and had a previous battalion command assignment in US Army Pacific, where I had both RA soldiers and AGR soldiers in my battalion. The catch is that all of these were within RA units.

The AGR allowed me to be more of a father to my son and husband to my wife than any Regular Army (RA) deployment could ever have. The *average* AGR assignments offer better working hours than the average RA assignments (*keep in mind, these are my experiences. A different person may have different experiences)*. For example, many soldiers and civilians in Reserve Component (RC) units (and Active Component units that work RC issues) leave work for the day between 4 and 6 p.m. if not earlier. However, the mindset is much different in the Regular Army. Most RA soldiers do not work according to the clock. The mentality is more of a 'leave when the work is done' mindset, and would you believe it if I told you the work is never done in the military (or any government office for that matter) because there is always something to improve upon. I speak from experience with both lifestyles whether I was deployed or not. Not to mention, the promotion system was far better in the AGR program than it was in the RA when I converted. For example, the promotion percentage from Captain to Major in the RA has consistently hovered around 80-85% for as long as I can remember. During the year that I joined the AGR program, the promotion percentage from Captain to Major in the AGR program was 99%. Out of 166 eligible Captains who went before the promotion board, 163 were selected for promotion to Major. This high percentage rate is in large part because most RA officers are squared away (or at least they are properly trained) at their current grade. Not to take anything away from the RC, but the RA officers have only one life – the Army life.

The RC soldier, specifically the ones who are part of the troop program unit (TPU), normally puts their civilian life first and their Army life second. This is because their civilian life and civilian job are the things that put the bacon on the table and pay the bills. A TPU soldier only works one weekend a month and two weeks per summer (on average), although many in key leadership positions work much more, and often for free on their own personal time while not on any type of pay-order. But for the RA officer, the Army is their primary job. They must be squared away on even the small things like ensuring their promotion packets are flawless. Completing the required training and schooling may be the best example. As noted, when an RA soldier needs to complete a required schooling for their current grade, the Army PCS's the soldier's entire family to that new duty station so the soldier can complete that training. However, when an RC soldier (remember TPU, not AGR) requires a certain training for their respective grade, that soldier must complete that training in their own free time while continuing to perform their full-time civilian employment. It is understandable why priorities may ultimately be different between the two soldiers. One prioritizes their civilian occupation over their military requirements while the other leans into everything the Army has to offer them.

Although the AGR soldier falls within the Reserve Component (RC), there are clearly two distinct breeds: those with the active duty mindset and those with the TPU mindset. Many AGR soldiers who convert from the TPU program, where they only drilled one weekend per month, are professionals and do very well. But there is certainly a sizeable amount who, after converting from TPU to AGR, still manage to be wired where their work ethic is not quite up to par with their fellow AGR soldiers who take everything seriously. This will look like one having more of the 'work until the mission is complete' mentality while the other 'works until the duty day/weekend drill is over' mentality.

RC officers (TPU, not AGR) have received almost automatic promotion to the rank of Lieutenant Colonel (a direct quote from a previous USARC G1 Human Resources Chief) as long as they have completed their intermediate level education (ILE) and have no *bad paper* in their official file (i.e., letters of reprimand filed). This is proof that an RC officer can receive many more center of mass (COM) OER ratings (an 'average' rating, that is neither good nor bad) than an RA officer and still have a good chance for promotion on the board. The USAR has not met its 'select objective' promotion quota for its TPU officers for several years. If the select objective is not met, this simply means the promotion board was not a 'best qualified' board, but simply a 'fully qualified' promotion board which means everyone who competed for the promotion completed the minimum amount of education for that grade and held the previous rank for the minimum amount of time.

This is not the case for the AGR promotion boards, however. The AGR promotion boards have met their select objective every year which means the board is truly a 'best qualified' versus 'fully qualified' board. Essentially, this means that each year there are AGR officers who are fully qualified (with the requisite amount of military and civilian education, time in grade at the previous rank, successful performance in key and developmental (KD) and branch qualifying (BQ) assignments at the previous grade), but still do not get selected for promotion because the 'select objective' was reached and a 'cut-line' had to be drawn. All those who fell below the cut-line were denied the promotion even though they knocked requirements out of the park. AGR officers must have some above center of mass (ACOM) ratings (better than average) to get promoted or they will risk falling below the cut-line.

Likewise, *all* RA officers *must* have some ACOM ratings to get promoted. There is only a 'fully qualified' promotion system from Second Lieutenant to First Lieutenant, but from Captain and higher it is a 'best qualified' promotion system in the RA. I have seen many good officers get passed over in the RA because of 'average files.' An average file in the RA will place you in the 'gray area' of the promotion zone. Unfortunately, with an 80% promotion rate for Major (this is lower for Lieutenant Colonel and even lower for Colonel) many officers in the 'gray area' do not make it. With the much higher percentages than the RC has, one is left to believe that the 'gray area' in the RC will still get you promoted. I have no verifiable proof, but the percentages may just speak for themselves. 99% in the RC were promoted from Captain to Major, but yet only 85% moved up for the same rank when I was promoted to Major in the RA in 2003.

I am very surprised, however, to admit that the times are changing. In the years 2006 and 2007, we began to see dramatic changes in this trend that have never been seen before. The AGR has recently developed new business practices that have caused their almost automatic promotions to drop considerably and lag behind the Active Component. The AGR no longer conducts its promotions simultaneously and in conjunction with TPU soldiers which had allowed the AGR to receive the better end of the stick by receiving high promotion rates when competing against their fellow TPU candidates who had fewer opportunities to perform at the same level. In other words, quality now trumps quantity. It doesn't matter if you are in the office every day. You can't just fake it for a weekend drill anymore. AGRs now have promotion boards solely for AGRs while TPUs have promotion boards solely for TPUs making it more fair for both categories. Not to mention, the AGR program began allowing Lieutenant Colonels to remain on active duty beyond their Mandatory Removal Date causing this population to rise leading to the promotion rates at the higher levels to be reduced. The bottom line is that additional rigor has been added to the AGR promotion process. AGR officers now must perform at higher levels, seek out the tougher jobs and do well by earning regular above center of mass (ACOM) reports to be competitive for promotion. This is much more in line with the way RA officers have lived for years.

These new AGR promotion initiatives are nothing new to the AGR officer who grew up in the RA system or to the AGR officer who may have grown up in the TPU system but has always had a high work ethic. But it is certainly new and a huge eye-opener to the AGR officer who grew up in the TPU system and continues to have a TPU mindset of putting their military career second. I do want to caveat that in many cases, a TPU's civilian job needs to come first. Being a first responder (such as doctors and nurses in busy hospitals, police officers, FBI agents, and other law enforcement) may make it difficult to prioritize military calls. Those who own their own small private businesses where the business may fail in their absence will surely put that business that provides for their family ahead of miliary obligations. The list goes on. The only problem is if they display this lackadaisical and under-performing attitude in their duties, they will then come across as an under-performer who chooses not to give 100% to their military duties or to their military career. I will reiterate that I am not generalizing and categorizing all TPU officers as having a 'TPU mindset.' Having served in the RC system as an AGR, TPU, and IMA, I have met many TPU and IMA officers who are the finest professionals I have ever worked with. I would trust them with any mission and with my life easily. I know this just as I know of many RA officers who I am still surprised ever made it on active duty, but somehow continue to receive promotions when they should be chaptered out. It is my opinion that the true cut-line that tells if an officer is squared away or not is 1. if they were selected for Battalion and/or Brigade Command from a Centralized Selection List/Board (CSL) and 2. if they performed well in that Command position. It is a very safe bet that someone who has successfully completed Battalion and/or Brigade Command (whether RA, TPU, or AGR) is a squared away officer capable of handling lots of responsibility in an outstanding manner.

PROMOTION PROTOCOL (2017-2022)

Throughout my military career, I have had the privilege of sitting on 12 different promotion boards, where I was permitted to, for lack of better words, 'peek behind the curtain' to see how the system *really* works. This opportunity gave me the invaluable experience of seeing what a strong file looks like and what an officer should or should not do throughout their career to improve their chances of promotion. Having spent my entire career spread between both the Active Component and Reserve Component, I have had the opportunity to work for (as a subordinate), with (as a teammate), and over (as a supervisor) Active Component soldiers, Reserve Component soldiers from both the U.S. Army Reserve and National

Guard, as well as U.S. government civilians and civilian contractors. Additionally, having served in two different joint Combatant Commands, three tours in the Pentagon where one was with Congress, and three separate combat deployments that were all joint and coalition related, I also had the opportunity to work closely with our other U.S. service components, U.S. governmental Departments (other than DoD), as well as our coalition partner nations from other countries. These experiences, namely the promotion boards, where I viewed thousands and thousands of files for promotion (one promotion board can easily have 5,000 candidates' files alone), has shown me that there are common themes or trends that a successful candidate for promotion will have.

Every promotion board is truly different because of the human aspect. If the process consisted of inputting a candidate's personnel file into a computer system and allowing the computer to evaluate each assignment and OER received and school attended, then there might possibly be a certain amount of consistency based on the parameters set within the program. However, that is not the case. Our current system consists of actual people who convene together at

Human Resources Command (HRC) for a period of time to manually review each candidate's personnel file consisting of their Officer Record Briefs (ORBs), Officer Evaluations Reports (OERs), among other documents within their file. If all promotion boards had the same exact board members every single time, then there might also be a certain amount of consistency. But that is not the case either. We say each promotion board is different because each board will convene a different panel of board members who are charged with voting the files and a different panel of live/human board members will inevitably bring their own individual biases with them and subconsciously use those biases in their ratings.

Whether we want to admit it or not, we all have certain biases that can affect the way we view and rate a candidate's file. While some people have biases based on skin color, others have biases based on gender. While some will have biases based on body composition (where a person in great shape may be biased towards someone they perceive as overweight by the naked eye), others will have biases based on the branch (where a combat arms officer may assume another officer is more squared away than a non-combat arms officers or vice versa). And still others will have biases against someone serving in a non-deployable/TDA unit (where they will favor someone who is currently serving in a deployable/MTOE unit over the candidate in the non-deployable unit, even if the candidate in the deployable unit has a lower ranked file from the assumption that the candidate in the deployable unit is working harder). The bottom line here is that the human aspect where board members bring their personal biases into the board process with them is something we cannot control. Once the board member goes into their cubicle to review a file and cast their vote, there is no one looking over their shoulder to tell them the logic they are applying may not be fair to all candidates.

There are a few minor safeguards, but none are anywhere near foolproof. The biggest safeguard is the use of the aberrant rule where if two board members have a large enough divergence in their voting of the same file, then those two board members will have to revote that file a second time in an attempt to get those two board members to come to a closer spread. However, there is nothing preventing those two board members from casting the same exact vote the second time around. The best saving grace that I have found that gives me faith in the process is the fact that it is surprisingly coincidental that the average board member, regardless of what walk of life they come from, will usually have similar mindsets and thought processes with regard to what they believe a successful officer and a successful career-track should look like.

Board members, at least for officer promotions, are usually 1-star and 2-star Generals, with a 2-star or 3-star serving as the President of the Board. There may be a couple Colonels on the board, but these Colonels will be 'Branch-Qualified' (BQ) and 'Key and Developmental' (KD) complete Colonels, which means they will not be brand new Colonels but senior Colonels who have already completed both Brigade Command (or a Brigade Command equivalent if they serve in a functional area) and are Senior Service College graduates. These Colonels are ready for promotion to General Officer at any time. With a board consisting of all Generals, or those ready to be a General, it is easy to understand that these individuals will view a candidate's file similarly, because the average General Officer has had a similar and successful 'cookie cutter' career path as other Generals where they started as a Platoon Leader, then Battalion (BN) Staff, then Company (CO) Commander (CDR), then BN or Brigade

(BDE) Staff, then BN XO, then some type of broadening assignment in either a functional area or a graduate program to get a Master's degree. Then these individuals return to complete another leadership position with soldiers, before BN CMD, BDE CMD, Chief of Staff, etc. These are the types of 'premier' leadership assignments that can lead to General Officer.

However, the lesser desired assignments (still very important, but that do not necessarily lead to General Officer) may include those with the vague wording that do not send the signal that you were in-charge of anything such as: "Assistant to the Assistant Special Projects LNO (i.e., Liaison) Staff Officer." With too many titles like this under your belt, you may not get selected for BN CMD. Without a successful BN CMD, you may not get selected for promotion to full-bird Colonel (at least not in the Active Component) which means you will never sit on a promotion board to offer your insight into promoting our officer corps to the next level. These General Officers, with their "General Officer mindset," who comprise the board, will often have similar criteria that they believe makes a file more competitive than others. I cannot speak for all General Officers, but I can tell you that the criteria I hold in high regard when voting a file, to give it a score between 1 and 6+, are (but not limited to):

- **Command**.

This means that you are Branch Qualified (BQ) and Key and Developmental (KD) complete at your current grade. If you have not completed a command position or the requisite position for your grade, it implies you are not quite ready for the next level. This would look like CO CMD for a Captain, BN XO for a Major (as a "hard KD") or BN or BDE OPS Officer for a Major (as a "soft KD"), BN CMD for a Lieutenant Colonel, and BDE CMD for a Colonel. Many senior leaders may have the mindset that while only one KD assignment makes you KD complete, it is most preferred to complete a hard KD assignment (i.e., CO/BN/BDE Command, XO, etc.) to be most competitive. If you are not fortunate enough to get selected for a hard KD assignment (because these assignments may entail getting selected from a Centralized Selection Board or from several different interviews by the Senior Rater where only the top candidate is selected), then it is highly recommended to do all you can to at least complete two soft KD assignments. These may be easier to secure as there are fewer interviews to compete for (i.e., BN/BDE OPS and similar positions) to keep you competitive with those who were fortunate to land the hard KD assignment. Having been selected for a command gives a board member the confidence and reassurance that the candidate has a strong file because it means a previous 'Command Board' has already gone through the same exact process to review this candidate's file. That previous board apparently granted this candidate a high enough score to be selected for command, which means it's safe to assume that this candidate will have a strong file even before beginning to view the first document.

- **Evaluations**.

There is a very limited amount of time to review each file. It honestly may be only two to four minutes per file to complete the estimated quota of files for each day of the board. Depending on the number of files to be voted on, a board can last anywhere between one to four weeks to complete the entire process and finish on time. I've had to be more selective than ever in terms of what I review. Otherwise, there is no way to review each entire file. When I am in the hot seat to complete file evaluations, I believe the Senior Rater portion of the OER is arguably one of the more important items to view. Focus areas of the Senior Rater's portion include:

a) Senior Rater's *first* sentence: Did the Senior Rater quantify the candidate in the first sentence and how strong is this quantification? Did this quantification contain any preferred *exclusive* verbiage such as: #1 of XYZ…, or the best at…. or top 1% of ABC...?
b) Senior Rater's *last* sentence: How strong of a 'recommendation to promote' did the Senior Rater use in the *last* sentence? Did the Senior Rater say something along the lines of promote with peers, promote ahead of peers, or must promote below the zone?
c) Senior Rater's labeling: Is the OER an Above Center of Mass / Most Qualified (ACOM / MQ), i.e., 'Top Block' or a Center of Mass / Highly Qualified / or Qualified (COM / HQ / Qualified)? It is well understood that everyone cannot get a Top Block, so the verbiage in the first and last sentences take on added importance to relay to the board that although the labeling may only reflect a COM, the OER still has a Top Block write-up. Just note, you cannot receive all COMs and expect to remain competitive, you have to show a *heartbeat* which means you have a

healthy number of Top Blocks, and that your file is not *flat-lined* where you have mostly all COMs with no heartbeat. As with a medical patient, if you are flat-lined with no heartbeat, that means you are (or at least your file is) dead.

d) Senior Rater's comment on your potential: Is the Senior Rater painting a clear picture in as few words as possible to highlight the candidate's strong potential for promotion to the *next* higher rank? There may be instances where a Rater is simply copying a candidate's support form verbatim telling me how many widgets were produced on the assembly line during this last rating period without highlighting any potential for the next higher grade. It is a clear *hidden* signal that you are only average at best if a Rater is telling me how many widgets you produced as opposed to strongly and vigorously telling me how you are their #1 choice to advance to the next grade.

e) Senior Rater's recommendation for your next three jobs: Are the next three positions that your Senior Rater is recommending you for only soft Staff level jobs or strong leadership positions where you are in-charge of soldiers? The stronger recommendations include: Commander, Chief of Staff, XO to a Principle (i.e., XO to a "King Maker" position such as a 3- or 4-star, etc.).

- **Senior Service College (SSC).**

This is for Lieutenant Colonels and Colonels, but similarly to being selected for command. It sends the message that your file has already been reviewed by a previous 'SSC Board' and that the board has already selected your file out of thousands of other candidates which helps make me automatically favorable towards your file before reviewing it.

- **Other Leadership Positions Held.**

Obviously, Command is the best job to have, but you cannot expect to serve as a Commander your entire career. There are many other broadening assignments and support positions that help to make a good well-rounded officer. Other than Command, the best positions are still those that show you were in-charge of something (whether people or equipment) with titles of Deputy Commander, Chief of Staff, Director, Commandant, Division Chief, Branch Chief, etc. If not in-charge, then at least were you the top assistant to someone very senior, such as a 3- or 4-star King Maker, where you had the title of: Executive Officer, Aide de Camp, Military Assistant to a 3- or 4-star, etc.

- **Deployments**.

We have been a "Nation at war" consistently now for over two decades. If you were already in, at least, your 3rd or 4th assignment, by the 2020 timeframe, and have never deployed, that could inadvertently send a bad message that you may have been *hiding* from a deployment. This is unfortunate because we do not have complete control over our assignments and we only go where the military sends us. But keeping in mind that the board members are typically Generals who have worked the hard KD jobs in leadership positions where they were in-charge of soldiers and have several deployments under their belt, they tend to fall victim to assumptions. To them, anyone who has served for over 10 years without a deployment, especially if they served during the peak deployment period (when we had regular deployments to Iraq and Afghanistan), can come across as someone intentionally trying to avoid deploying.

- **Units Served In**.

As stated, we go where the military sends us. But it is fair to say that a board member may favor a candidate who has done well while serving in certain units that are respected (i.e., deployable/MTOE units with soldiers as opposed to non-deployable/TDA units with lots of civilians). Do not misunderstand. I am not implying it is a bad thing to serve in a TDA organization. The Pentagon, White House, Congress, NATO, joint Combatant Commands, and many other TDA organizations can certainly improve your file. The key is to show you are a well-rounded officer with many different experiences. Your file will have a negative look if it shows you have primarily rotated from one soft non-deployable TDA unit to another similar unit where you work jobs with soft duty titles that have little to no leadership or responsibility. All CO CDRs in the military cannot be crammed into the 82nd Airborne Division with the duty title of 'commander.' Someone has to be the CO CDR of the Recruiting BN or the Basic Training BN or the HHC CO CDR of the non-deployable Schoolhouse. What is important is that you adhere to the ole' adage of "bloom where you are planted." This saying speaks to the notion that "even flowers grow in the desert." So, wherever you are assigned by the military, you have the ability to perform your best to earn the best possible rating to continue advancing.

- **Master's Degree**.

Earning a Master's degree, as well as completing additional military schooling, sends a clear message that you do not sit idle and that you are always trying to improve, learn, and be the best soldier/officer possible.

- **Mobile**.

Another negative look (similar to sitting idle and being complacent) is homesteading in the same area without PCSing to different units to gain different experiences. There are some military occupational specialties (MOS) and branches (i.e., Civil Affairs, Psychological Operations, Rangers, and several others) that have limited assignment options because there are not that many of those types of units and positions in their field, so it is more common for them to homestead in the same area. If they can complete the requisite BQ/KD assignments for their grade, deploy, and complete other requirements to continually improve (think schooling), then it is not an issue for them to continue serving at the same installation without PCSing frequently. However, for the soldier with a more basic or common branch/MOS where there is no shortage of options, it is not a good look to attempt to homestead in the same area. You may be inadvertently sending a poor signal to the board that you are not mobile and not willing to PCS to different locations, and thereby failing to gain valuable experiences to become a well-rounded officer.

- **Uniform**.

The official DA photo is no longer included in the promotion board file, but this doesn't mean there aren't several items throughout the file that allow a board member to form a mental picture of the candidate. There is actually quite a bit that is readily accessible without taking much time to locate. For example, the OER shows the candidates height and weight on the first page and the ORB shows the types of units served in, the level of education, awards earned, and military schooling completed. All these items combined paint a clear picture as to whether a soldier is lazy and takes up space working the easy jobs or if they are easily within body-fat standards and motivated to work the hard jobs. It is easy to tell who shows a strong desire to continue their education and not sit idle or be complacent. Regarding awards, if a person is a Lieutenant Colonel and their highest award is only an Army

Commendation Medal (ARCOM), that can send a message if they have served for 15 years and have PCS'd a couple times as a field grade officer, yet their leadership has never thought enough of them to give them a Meritorious Service Medal (MSM). The same goes for a senior Captain who has never earned an ARCOM.

This above listing, of criteria that I hold in high regard when voting a file is not an all-inclusive list and it is not necessarily in rank order. If all things were equal, then I would feel more comfortable saying that it is rank ordered for *my* preference. But we know all things are not equal. For example, some command positions have the duty title of 'Commander' but the OER shows that the Rater is also of the 'same' rank. The duty description may show that the position only supervises a couple individuals within a non-deployable/TDA organization. This would clearly not be the normal type of command that would grant a 'KD completion' and would be more of an 'OIC' type of position vs. a true 'Command' position. You also need to consider the type of board you are sitting on. You may need to approach an Army Reserve (USAR) board differently than a Regular Army (RA) board. There is a popular phrase in ROTC that says "a command is a command is a command." This may be true for some in the USAR, but certainly not true for anyone in the RA.

In the RA, the onion is peeled back for most every category. For example, the question can be asked in the USAR "did you complete Senior Service College (SSC)?" If the answer is "yes," then we can move on to the next question. But in the RA if you answer "yes, I completed SSC," then we start to ask follow up questions. We ask "Ok, that's great, but did you complete it resident or non-resident?" In the USAR, you would not be penalized. There may be one or two USAR board members who would be curious, but definitely not a majority of the board members. Meanwhile, all of the RA board members would want to know if you completed the resident course or non-resident course.

Command would be an even better example. In the USAR, the question can be asked "did you complete a command?" If the answer is "yes," then most of the USAR board members would be satisfied if you successfully completed command and received a decent OER. However, in the RA if you answer "yes, I completed command," we then peel back the onion and ask "Ok, that's great, but was it a deployable/MTOE command or a non-deployable/TDA command?" If you answer "MTOE," we continue peeling back the onion inquiring "Ok since it was a deployable MTOE command, did you actually deploy while serving as a commander?" If you answer "yes, I deployed while serving as commander." We go even deeper inquiring "Ok since you did deploy, did your unit actually go outside the wire or were you a 'fobbet' where you stayed inside the wire the entire time during your deployment?" I was being a little facetious to exaggerate my point, because obviously, a board member cannot talk directly to a candidate, during their board review, nor would they have the time to do so. But hopefully this explains that the RA candidate's file may be scrutinized a bit more in certain areas than the USAR candidate's file.

During a promotion board (and SSC and Command Boards), a candidate's file is ranked from a 1 to a 6+. I want you to think back to that college class that gave you a B+ as a final grade. The same principle takes place on these promotion boards where you can score a 3- or a 5+. With that said, there are 17 potential ranks that someone can receive. A score of '1' means the candidate is not only not recommended for promotion, but also must go before a 'Show Cause Board' (a board convened by the candidate's parent unit) where the candidate must explain why they should be allowed to remain in the service. A 'cut line' is typically voted on by the board members on the first day. The line could be between any numbers ultimately agreed upon by the board. Let's assume that the cut line is drawn between 2 and 3. A score of '2' means the candidate is not recommended for promotion. There is no adverse action taken for scoring a 2 (as with having to undergo a Show Cause Board for scoring a 1), it simply means your file is removed and you will not be included in the final 'racked and stacked' list to ultimately see if you make the 'cut line' for promotion (or Command or SSC depending on what type of board it was). Meanwhile, all candidates with an average score (from all board members) of 3- through 6+ are 'racked and stacked' for consideration for promotion.

The Army's Operational Research System Analysis (ORSA; Functional Area 49) officers will crunch the numbers for each board to determine the required number of officers to be selected for promotion based on the Army's end-strength and other factors. This number informs HRC where to draw the line to determine how many candidates on the racked and stacked list will be promoted. To score a perfect score of 6+, the candidate would have to check all the (imaginary) boxes a board member has in their head such as having received ACOM ratings along with a deployment or having completed a hard KD Command assignment and other respectable leadership or high-profile positions (Chief of Staff, XO, etc.). However, if the candidate completed no KD positions, no deployments, and received all COMs, then they would still qualify to be racked and stacked. It may just so happen to be a lower score and they would be least likely to make the cut. This brings me back to the human aspect of promotion boards, command boards, and SSC boards, and illuminates how the board member's biases and subjectivity can have a huge impact. If there are two files that are almost identical, but the same board member votes one file a 5 and the next file a 5+, that minor difference could be the difference if a candidate makes the list or not.

Almost my entire career, since being commissioned in May 1992, has been on active duty. Additionally, during the four years of enlisted service in the National Guard, I acquired approximately four and a half months of additional active-duty time for such schools as Basic Training, Advanced

Individual Training, and portions of the Reserve Component (RC) Sapper School where I was on full-time orders. Even though I graduated college and was commissioned in May 1992, my active duty start date was adjusted (or rather backdated) to January 1992. So, although I was technically in the Reserve Component (RC) as an AGR officer, I had served on active duty every day since my commissioning and have essentially lived the same life of the average Regular Army (RA) officer (up until I pinned on the star of Brigadier General). Army Reserve soldiers serve in four basic capacities:

1. Troop Program Unit (TPU). A majority of Reserve Component (RC) soldiers are Drilling Reservists or Traditional Reservists who participate in unit training activities on a part-time basis, usually one weekend a month and two weeks of annual training per year. (Note: The National Guard refers to its 'TPU soldiers' as 'M-Day' soldiers).

2. Individual Mobilization Augmentee (IMA). IMAs are trained individuals assigned to an Active Component (AC), Selective Service System, or Federal Emergency Management Agency

(FEMA) organization's billet which must be filled on, or shortly after, mobilization. IMAs participate in training activities on a part-time basis with an AC unit in preparation for recall in a mobilization. IMAs typically serve a minimum of 70 days per year up to serving on a full-time basis of 365 days per year provided the organization has the funding to pay all associated costs for the IMA soldier to serve. The USAR will pay up to 70 days of duty per year, and the active-duty organization can elect to fund, out of its budget, any additional days beyond the 70 that the USAR funds.

3. Individual Ready Reserve (IRR). IRR soldiers provide a manpower pool composed of soldiers who have had training and previously served on active duty or in the reserves. They are not obligated to drill, conduct annual training, or participate in any military activities (except for periodic Muster activities) unless activated by Presidential Reserve Call Up. If they do not serve enough time throughout the year, they will not accrue a 'good year' that will be creditable towards retirement. You need 20 'good years' to qualify for retirement, but even after these

individuals call it quits, they remain in the manpower pool to be 'called up' to serve if needed for any emergency.

4. Active Guard/Reserve (AGR). AGR soldiers serve on active duty for the purpose of organizing, administering, recruiting, instructing, or training the reserve component units. They receive the same benefits as active component (AC) soldiers.

You may be wondering what justified my promotion to Brigadier General. Although difficult, the question has come up before. Although a promotion to General Officer is somewhat of a defining moment and point of success, this promotion was also a bittersweet moment. The *sweet* part of a promotion is obvious. However, the AGR program only goes up to Colonel/O-6. There are no GOs in the AGR program. Because of this, I had to exit the AGR program altogether to move up. I would enter either the TPU or IMA programs where TPU positions are part-time while the IMA program has both part-time and full-time positions.

Getting promoted to General Officer (GO) is unlike other promotions. Up to the rank of Colonel, you are promoted first and then assigned a position afterwards. USAR GO promotions on the other hand are directly linked to the position. To be promoted to GO, you must be favorably selected in two separate boards that take place almost simultaneously: the U.S. Army Reserve (USAR) General Officer Assignment Advisory Board (GOAAB) and the General Officer Promotion Selection Board (GOPSB). You will not be notified unless you were also selected for a specific GO position *in addition to* being selected for promotion. Even if you made the promotion list (which there is no way for you to know), it wouldn't be executed without a position the boards have in mind. In my case, I was selected for a TPU position, as the Deputy Commanding General (DCG) of the 80th Training Command in Richmond, VA. My choices were to either refuse the promotion and continue in the AGR program as a full-time Colonel on active duty or to accept the promotion and transfer from AGR (full-time status) to TPU (part-time status). I would also be remiss if I did not say that because I had over 20 years of active duty, I could have also turned down the promotion and chosen to retire altogether.

My attitude was always an *'up or out'* attitude as opposed to an idle, content, complacent one. When you stop trying to be your very best and become content with where you are, then it is time to retire and step aside to make room for someone else who 'does have' that burning desire to reach for the stars. Our soldiers deserve that at the very least from their leaders. Accepting this promotion meant I promoted myself out of active duty, at least for that near-term period. However, RC GOs in TPU assignments can

perform 179 days on active-duty per year that the USAR will pay for and perform an additional 179 days on active-duty per year that the Regular Army/Active Component covers. These just need to be requested and approved through the USAR and through the AC respectively. Since my entire officer career (from Second Lieutenant through Colonel) was on active duty, my intention was always to work the maximum number of active-duty days the Army would allow.

If I was ever unable to perform at least half the year on active duty, I would then reevaluate my options and decide to retire considering I would make more money each month in retirement than I would by performing only one-weekend per month drill and no other military service. In my case however, my one saving grace, is that I had already completed over 20 years of active federal service (AFS) which meant that even if my last job was in a part-time TPU status, my retirement would still be an active-duty retirement where I would begin drawing and receiving a retirement check the very next month. Since I was always so good with saving money, investing money, and accruing a sizeable nest egg with no bills or debt to my name, it made the decision to remain in uniform, even in a part time TPU status, much easier to make. Obviously, I would have loved to have had *all* full-time positions, but I was very fortunate to have only served in one part time TPU position during my entire career considering I straddled both the AC and RC during my career. Additionally, during this one part time TPU position as Deputy Commanding General of the 80th Training Command, I spent one of my two years in the position on active duty by volunteering to serve on multiple promotion boards and volunteering to serve as the

Investigating Officer on multiple back-to-back 15-6 investigations (where I completed multiple full-time assignments to investigate Colonels and below accused of violating the UCMJ). The full-time salary was nice, but that was not my goal. My primary goal was always to accrue as much active-duty time as possible to increase my active-duty retirement percentage-pay. After completing this 24-month tour as DCG, I then served in two successive full time IMA positions, one in Hawaii and one in Germany, where I was on active duty status once again prior to retiring on May 31, 2022.

Promotion to Brigadier General

PART III – SHOW ME THE MONEY

"This is the fifth planet from the sun. Yes, Fletcher?" Ken Jennings (Alex Trebek's replacement on Jeopardy) turns his attention to me standing among the contestants. My buzzer was still hot in hand as I answered. In a split second, I went into the archives of elementary school to find the answer. The riddle popped up in my head as I read along: My Very Earthly Mother Just Served Us Nine Pizzas. "What is Jupiter?" I confidently call out in the nick of time. "That is correct! Where would you like to go next?" Ken asked as eyes reverted to me and the applause started to die down. "Let's stay with this same category of 'Useless Things I Learned in Grade School for 400, Ken."

If only it was this easy to cash out on irrelevant information… Unfortunately, I have never been on Jeopardy and strongly doubt that this question is in contention for the big screen. I have so many of those same caliber factoids baked into my brain from years of rote memorization, such as being able to recite the colors of the rainbow in order by reciting the name Roy G. Biv, (using the first letter of each) to represent Red Orange Yellow Green Blue Indigo Violet, and so many other useless factoids I'll never use. Our current school system is broken. In grade school, we can learn algebra, geometry, trigonometry, and calculus (along with other subjects that I've forgotten) that we will almost never use outside of a school setting. Meanwhile, the benefits of financial literacy may come in handy on an almost daily basis. After making it this far in life, I realized that the bare minimum to teach in schools is financial literacy, but this doesn't even make the cut. Just think about it. Graduating high school or even college is not a guaranteed way to achieve financial success. People are spending thousands upon thousands of dollars just to live paycheck to paycheck. Our only badge for completion seems to be more debt. And here I am left with a few useless math formulas that I will remember for a lifetime. It would be invaluable if our school system taught money principles in primary and secondary school. Instead of memorizing things that can be found with a quick google search, schools should prioritize the practical principles of budgeting. In today's time, you can be on welfare or making 6-figures and still fall victim to poor spending habits. Broke doesn't discriminate as much as we like to believe it does.

I was very fortunate to have picked up some financial hacks along the way. Contrary to popular belief, I learned more outside the classroom than I would have ever imagined. Coming from such humble beginnings, you can learn just how far the mighty dollar can go. Once you gain an appreciation for green, the only thing to do is make more. I learned at an early age the power multiple streams of income working for you can have. If I told you this was a financial literacy book, would you believe me? Well in this chapter, we are about to change that thought.

WHEELS UP (1979-1988)

At age 11, I practically started taking care of myself. I bought my own clothes, a lot of my family's food, and helped my mother pay the household bills. Between the ages of 11 and 20, I consistently held at least two jobs at a time. I realized how good a feeling it was to have some extra pocket change. I told myself then that I would never have a money problem again as long as I had something to say about it. Little did I know I was learning the skill of diversification right then and there.

You remember those pedals I gifted myself? This seemed like the pot of gold at the end of a rainbow. I realized that I could put these pedals and the rest of my bike to good use. I started with two large paper routes that weaved all through Fredericksburg. From shear consistency, I managed to upgrade my bicycles over and over again. I graduated to a moped, and then upgraded that one to another. By the age of 15, I moved to the big leagues by buying a '77 Firebird (which was only eight years old at that time), for $2,000. I managed to purchase this car even before I was old enough to get a driver's license in the state of Virginia. It was a great feeling to pay for the car in one full payment, as well as pay the monthly car insurance on my own.

Paperboy evolved to dishwasher and busboy which then provided opportunities to become a short-order cook and ice cream maker. I jumped over to try my hand at salesmanship and telemarketing. By the age of 17, I championed delivery driving for an office supply store which evolved into loading and driving trucks for the same newspaper company where I got my first taste of independence. With a little loyalty mixed in with grit, I was promoted to assistant district manager of the newspaper company. Who would have thought that I would oversee a group of paperboys who looked a lot like me just a few years after the fact? I paired this new responsibility with the function of a security guard and finally rounded things out as a soldier in the Army to close out a formidable 10-year stint as a contributor to society before I upped the ante. I wasn't afraid of work as long as the price was right. For what it's worth, I have excellent references from most all of my previous employers. By most, I mean all except one.

I remember I landed a job at Shoney's restaurant where I was hired to be a dishwasher at age 16. For those of you who don't have a few gray hairs or have spent some time in the South, Shoney's is a full-service restaurant that prides itself in being the family dining destination with friendly service and delicious food. Nowadays, they have been on a steady decline with fierce competition in the restaurant space. Anyway, back in 1986, the manager on my first day gave me an apron and a scrub brush. He walked me outside and showed me the dumpster behind the restaurant. He went on to explain to me how I would need to scrub the outside of the dumpster clean at the start of every shift then report to him for his inspection afterwards. He proceeded to walk back into the restaurant and closed the door behind him. Now maybe you can help me with this, but how in the world would scrubbing the oil, dirt, grease, and grime off a dumpster fit into the job description of a dishwasher, let alone meet the needs and wants of the customers that frequented that establishment? If you thought the 'ask' (or rather, the manager's 'directive') was silly yourself, you wouldn't be surprised by what happened next. I immediately tossed the apron and scrub brush into the dumpster and hopped on my moped and rode across the busy intersection and got a job at a restaurant across the street where I was treated much better. I guess I can honestly say it was my worst job ever after a solid 5 minutes total on the clock. I will let you decide if you have seen worse, both by an employee and employer.

On February 27, 1988, I enlisted in the Army National Guard. I was only in my senior year of high school when I signed the papers. But I knew that I wanted to leave my neighborhood, go off to college and make something of myself and the National Guard offered the best opportunity to pay for college. I was only 17 at the time because my birthday would not come until that August. So, my mom did one of the biggest things she had ever done for me—besides giving birth—and signed special forms giving me permission to join. The two primary reasons I enlisted in the National Guard were the $2,000 entry bonus and the Montgomery G.I. Bill to pay for college.

FINANCIAL ADVANTAGE (1988-1992)

Growing up poor had finally paid off because I received lots of financial aid. Norfolk State University actually wrote me a personal check each semester. I believe the maximum amount one could have received from financial aid was approximately 80%, or at least that was the amount during the years I attended college. Because I was able to write down "ZERO" in the column entitled "Parents Annual Income," I received the maximum amount of financial aid. On top of that, the Virginia Army National Guard paid 50% of tuition if you attended a state university during the years I attended (it has since been increased to 100%). That's right. NSU wrote me a check for the excess 30% each semester. College is normally thought to be poor times, but I am convinced that I did my time, in poverty, years prior. To put it all together, I was receiving the following payments:

- 30% of excess tuition each semester in the form of personal check from NSU
- $150 per mo. from National Guard Drill Pay as an E-4 Specialist (keep in mind, this was 1988's pay rate)
- $160 per mo. from National Guard G.I. Bill
- $100 per mo. because I was enrolled in ROTC class (it is now $500 per month)
- $600 per mo. from my civilian job as a security guard ($5 per hour x 30 hours a week; for context, minimum wage in

1988 was only $3.35, so this was more than minimum wage)

Needless to say, I lived in a nice apartment off campus in the city of Virginia Beach, drove a nice car and always had money in my pocket. But I didn't stop there. A couple of my older sisters allowed me to literally grocery shop in their refrigerators for free with no questions asked. Incidentally, those particular sisters were always supportive of me and still are to this day. I will always have gratitude for them.

I graduated debt-free with no student loans from Norfolk State University in May 1992 and received a commission as a Second Lieutenant in the Regular Army (RA). I received my first branch choice of Transportation and my first duty preference for a duty assignment to Germany. After all these years, I was ahead of the curve and the best was yet to come.

THE BRASS TAX (1992-2022)

There are multiple ways to be successful in life. Earning a college degree immediately out of high school is probably the best way to jump start your career. However, college is not for everyone, and given the expensive costs of many colleges and universities, earning a college degree could actually set you back if you are not focused and do not have a plan. Now these are definitely rare cases, but they do exist. Some people may actually do much better joining the military right out of high school, to serve on active duty as an enlisted soldier, to first acquire the discipline needed in adulthood. Others may do better going to a vocational school to acquire a trade after high school such as plumbing, welding, etc. There are many trade schools that allow you to get paid during the program, graduate debt-free, and offer job-placement where the program finds you a job upon graduation. Regardless of what route you take, it is super helpful to have mentors along the way to both listen to you and offer constructive, experienced, helpful, and proven advice.

We have all heard the war stories of young adults graduating from college and going straight into debt. In many cases, people won't even graduate, only completing a couple of years towards a degree and still owing well over $100K in student loan debt with no college degree to show for it or *even worse*, a degree that is useless because of irrelevant skillsets acquired. You are now left with a very expensive degree but still unable to secure a job with four years into adulthood behind you. On the other hand, the individual who knew from the beginning that he or she was only a C student and knew that college was not for them chose instead to go against the grain. They join the military for one tour to acquire both more discipline and money for college. That person is now more mature and now has access to resources that will fund their way through college. They may even have a better understanding of what they would like to learn in college after having some real-life experience guide them. This individual is more likely to be focused and graduate on time with a goal and purpose in mind.

Alternatively, the D student who chooses a trade school right out of high school is also likely to complete this very short program debt-free in two years or less. They immediately enter the job market with skills that an employer is in high demand of and willing to pay top dollar for. Just four years later, this individual will have years of work experience in a respectable career as opposed to the college student who was never ready in the first place (financially or mentally), but instead has a whopping student loan and still no job. Just think about that opportunity cost for a second with respect to both time and money. Having said all this, my advice is *still* to go to an accredited college if you can afford it, to secure a degree, but to do it smartly and after having researched it thoroughly. For inspiration, look for the people who have the lifestyle that you aspire to have and work hard to get their attention. Take any advice and mentorship you can get and *act* unless you know for certain that college is not for you. Even then, know you have options outside of that.

Mentors who have been through this journey before can provide the best advice as they have already successfully navigated this minefield of choosing the right college for your goals. There is a great quote I picked up that says: "the cost of an education is great, but the cost of ignorance is much greater." Most high school juniors and seniors will not understand this until it is too late. They may be more inclined to choose a college that competes or compares to their friends and classmates, but not taking into account that their classmate may have parents who have the resources and means to simply write a check to the school to cover all fees. Meanwhile, you on the other hand could be saddling yourself in debt that may take decades to pay off whereby it causes you to live a less than fruitful life for the next 20 years. Never think that you don't have leverage. If there is a will, there is a way to get paid.

Mentorship does not stop once you find your path out of high school, it continues into adulthood and beyond. In fact, it becomes even more important as you progress through your career whether that career is deeply entrenched in the military or not. As I talk to (and mentor) young officers, several *nuggets of wisdom* that I like to emphasis are:

- **Dignity and Respect**.

What if everyone was treated with the utmost respect? Doing this is the most important thing in *my* opinion. I start to think of different leadership styles and how that ultimately impacts where something like treating others with dignity is ranked. You may have found many leaders who have a very strong 'Type-A' personality. They come across as over-bearing, aggressive, loud, brash, vulgar, and other traits less than flattering. This doesn't mean that they aren't extremely successful. In some (albeit rare) situations, this conduct may be necessary. Just think, a combat commander works up the courage in a bloody battle to tell his troops the next action. He yells over the cries of war to "charge – and take that hill!" knowing that a majority of his men will die in the exercise. In this scenario, there is no room for the men to second guess the leader and ask "why." There is no time to propose other options that *they* believe are safer. The commander has received orders from his superiors and he is simply carrying out those orders, and everyone involved must trust and understand that they are only one piece of a larger puzzle whereby the mission can only be accomplished if everyone does their part.

However, in normal *everyday/routine* duty, we are not "charging the hill," we are not putting our lives on the line, and we are simply performing more or less administrative functions to accomplish a mission. These aren't life or death combat situations. It may very well be an *average* Tuesday in the office. With that said, we definitely have the time and ability to treat everyone with dignity and respect. I have found that when soldiers and civilians are treated with dignity and respect, they are much more willing to work twice as hard for you, which only makes you and your mission that much more successful. I personally love it when everyone can come to work happy *and* go home happy. Regardless, you have to find what works best for you. Just know honey does a better job attracting flies than vinegar.

- **Hubris**.

The biggest most powerful U.S. Navy ship was sailing through the water and sees a small light ahead from another ship in its course. A young Lieutenant on the big Navy ship says over the mic to the person in its way, "This is the USS Lincoln. You are in our way. Change your course by 15 degrees to the North to avoid a collision." The other person says: "I am sorry, we were here first. You change course by 15 degrees to the South to avoid a collision." They keep going back and forth up the chain from the Lieutenant to the Commander to the Captain, and finally to the Admiral all repeating the same lines and threats. The Admiral gets on the mic and says very boldly with his chest stuck out: "This is Admiral So & So, and I command the Largest Fleet in the Entire U.S. Navy. I am ordering you to change your course by 15 degrees to the North immediately or we will blow you out of the water. Do you understand me!?" The other person calmly says: "Well Sir that is very impressive, and you certainly have a lot of power at your command. While we are only two very old men and an even older dog with us, but I have to warn you that we are a 'lighthouse,' so it is your call whether you want to change your course or not." This story always reminds me that we *can* fix ignorance, but we *cannot* fix arrogance.

This is humility in its purest form. You must avoid this crime of thinking you are better than everyone else. You must never forget where you came from. You must be a genuine 'Servant Leader.' Those that you lead can see right through you and will know if you care about them or not. No matter how big and bad you think you are, there is always someone out there who can humble you real quick. Avoid entitlement. Carry your *own* bags and open your *own* doors.

- **Teams and Trust**.

At the end of the day, the bare necessities to accomplish any mission are two-fold: teamwork and trust. You must never lie! If you choose to do so, your trust will be broken and teamwork destroyed. It will be an irreparable mess. The best way to build trust is through consistent behavior over a long period of time.

- **Micro-engage not Micro-manage**.

Your subordinates need to see that you are *present* and that you have their back. Surprisingly, the most common reason commanders get fired is not because they did something illegal, immoral, or unethical. The most common reasons commanders get fired is from *inaction,* by failing to take appropriate steps after something *usually* illegal, immoral, or unethical has been brought to their attention by a subordinate who trusted them to *engage* when they were supposed to. Don't micro-manage but maintain situational awareness and situational understanding. You must empower your subordinates and give them the room, freedom, and trust to accomplish the mission. They may just surprise you. Just because you have to hold everyone accountable because you are ultimately responsible doesn't mean you can't delegate and inspire accordingly.

- **Alcohol**.

When mentoring young military leaders, alcohol is *always* a point to remind them of. I have seen a few good officers taken down by their inability to control their alcohol. Regardless of how squared away you may be, even if you are the most polished individual in the entire organization, when you receive a driving under the influence (DUI) or driving while intoxicated (DWI) charge, the punishment is often taken away from your immediate commander in order for the first General Officer in your chain of command to chastise you. The punishment is usually an automatic General Officer Memorandum of Reprimand (GOMOR) that is filed in your permanent personnel file at Human Resources Command (HRC) that prevents you from future promotions. With regard to alcohol, "life is hard and it's way harder when you're stupid."

Each leader will have their own set of gems that they like to preach about based on their leadership style. There is no right or wrong set of morals or points of value that every officer must follow in any particular order. I've come to find that what works well for one may not work so well for another based on their individual style. Based on my personality and leadership style, I like to champion those nuggets of wisdom noted above, but simply trying to do the right thing and following the Golden Rule of treating everyone how you would want to be treated is usually a good start. Over time, you will eventually find your own way that works best for you. Let's not follow the *other* Golden Rule: "he who has the gold rules." This one will eventually cause you to fall on your face, or worse.

I always maintained a good relationship with the soldiers. I found it easy to relate with them since I was once enlisted and I tried never to just automatically treat them according to their rank. I always tried to treat them all like human beings. I could be mistaken but I like to think that I talk to Specialists and Sergeants (and all enlisted soldiers) the same way I do to senior officers who outrank me. My volume, tone, sincerity and respect to whomever I am talking to is the same. Many officers forget to treat enlisted soldiers in that manner.

I have found that treating all with dignity and respect is a 100% fool-proof way to both receive the best an individual has to offer, and to receive even more respect back in return. You can imagine that an enlisted soldier or junior-grade or mid-grade officer (who does all the legwork anyways) is pleasantly surprised when senior officers treat them with the best of intentions. I have found that they are so appreciative that they make it their life's work to take care of you and ensure you not only never fail but also to ensure you always appear successful.

THE INFLECTION POINT (2022)

Fast forward nearly 35 years of service, and everything is automatic. My total monthly salary I received prior to my retirement, in 2022, was *drumroll please* $18,922.78 including the monthly housing allowance if I lived off-base. However, I received $15,585.90 per month with no housing allowance (because I lived in on-post housing for free). This total amount was the sum of three separate allowances that a soldier receives monthly all in one check. Step into my office for the breakdown:

Base Pay was $14,445.60 per month. This was built up over time with no breaks in service. Experience pays in the military and since I had 34 years under my belt as an O-7, money was healthy. O-7 (Brigadier General) signifies the officer rank achieved over my tenure with the lowest being O-1 (which equals that of a Second Lieutenant) and highest being O-10 (which is a full-fledged four star General).

BAS (or basic allowance for subsistence) was $280.30 per month. Think of The Jungle Book's "bare necessities" when trying to stack up this income. This would offset my personal meals. All officers (O-1 through O-10) receive the same amount regardless of their rank. enlisted soldiers receive BAS in different amounts based on their rank.

BAH (or basic allowance for housing) for me would have been $3,336.88 per month in Stuttgart, Germany. This amount can range from $2,400-3,500 per month depending on where you live. You only receive this if you live off-post. On post, you can assume that everything from a housing perspective was covered. BAH is prorated based on the zip code you are assigned to because this value is tied to the cost of living in any particular area. If you were based in a rural location, expect to get an amount lower in the range and vice versa for urban areas. I resided in on-post housing in Stuttgart, Germany where there was no rent, but I did not receive any

BAH either. General Officers usually reside in on-post housing (not a law written in stone, but usually out of convenience to perform our required duties more easily) in order to have access to a secure (i.e., secret level) communications suite that's standard in General Officer housing. As you can imagine, a call with the Pentagon can't be as easy as picking up your cell phone from a speed dial. When duty called, it didn't matter if you were nestled in the comfort of your home. You needed viable and secret level channels of communication to carry out your duties 24-7.

COLA (or cost of living allowance) was $860 per month in Germany. COLA is given to all service members who live outside of the continental U.S. (OCONUS), in high cost of living areas. When I was assigned in Hawaii between 2010-2013 as a Lieutenant Colonel (LTC), my monthly COLA was $1,405.00 per month, because the cost of living is higher in Hawaii than Germany. Mind you, there are a few locations within continental bounds that had COLA as well (think New York City and Los Angeles), but those were few and far in between.

Put all of this together and we get a **monthly salary of $18,922.78** equaling an **annual $227,073**. I wanted to go ahead and include something representative for rent, so even though I wasn't technically securing BAH, that value was still representative. But wait, there's more! This six-figure salary did not account for:

- Free medical and dental
- Discount shopping in the Post Exchange (think heavily discounted BrandsMart USA or mini-Walmart)
- Discount auto insurance among other things through organizations that cater to the military officer
- Wardrobe savings by wearing a uniform daily instead of a suit
- The opportunity to live, work, and travel all over the world; and all other fringe benefits the military offers
- Adjustment for inflation *every* year to keep pace with the cost of living

That is a lot of money considering that I had *zero* credit card bills, student loans, or signature loans. To this day, I never use a conventional credit card. I can't even tell you the last time I paid a personal monthly credit card bill. Not to mention, my wife made her own money as a civil federal government employee (she went from GS-5 to GS-15 throughout her 21-and-a-half-year career), paid her own bills, and contributed to joint household bills. Both of our vehicles are paid in full. I have a 2022 530i xDrive BMW (quite the upgrade even from the Firebird back in the day), and Rhonda has a 2014 Range Rover Sport.

During my stint in the Army, traveling was my biggest pastime. In addition to living in four different cities in Germany (for a total of six years), to include: Mannheim, Frankfurt, Hanau, and Stuttgart, as well as living in Puerto Rico (for a total of three years) and living in Hawaii on two separate occasions (for a total of four and a half years), I have also visited (and most with my wife and son) the following countries and/or territories (and visiting many of them on multiple occasions, denoted with an '*'): on the African Continent: South Africa, Swaziland and Niger; on the European Continent: Spain*, France*, Portugal*, Switzerland, Italy*, Holland* (i.e. Netherlands as it is referred in Europe), Austria, Belgium, Denmark, England* (i.e. United Kingdom as it is referred in Europe), Iceland, Montenegro, Croatia, Greece*, Liechtenstein and of course Germany; on the Asian Continent; Kuwait, Iraq, Afghanistan, Singapore and Japan;

on the Australia and Oceania Continent: Guam*; on the South American Continent: Columbia; on the Central American Continent: Panama*, Belize and Costa Rica; in the Caribbean Sea of the North American Continent: Aruba, St. Thomas*, St. John*, St. Croix, Barbados, Bahamas*, Dominican Republic, Dominica*, St. Kitts, St. Lucia, Jamaica*, Cayman Islands* and Turks & Caicos; on the North American Continent: Canada, Mexico* and all over the U.S. mainland, including Alaska* and Hawaii*. And since I have deployed three times, with the military, I can also (reluctantly) say I have lived in Kuwait for six months, Iraq for 12 months, and Afghanistan for nine months.

I began investing in mutual funds as a Second Lieutenant in February 1993 contributing $500 per month. With every promotion I obtained, I increased these monthly contributions until I became a General Officer in February 2017. By that point, I was contributing $1,350 per month to mutual funds, index funds, and exchange-traded funds (ETFs). Additionally, I was also contributing $888 per month to the Thrift Savings Plan (TSP), through my military employment. That's $2,238 in aggressive growth investments per month that I prioritized over any other spending. The additional investments Rhonda made into her own TSP, through her government employment, are not factored into the amount above. After 24 years of contributions compounding on one another, from 1993 – 2017, I stopped making monthly contributions. I still have not touched (i.e., withdrawn) any of the investments, I simply have stopped adding to them and only relying on the *compounded interest* to grow the account annually and for the '*rule of 72*' to essentially double it in size roughly every 5-7 years (as we'll discuss later).

Do not misunderstand, there is a difference between being frugal and *wise* with your money. As a graduate of an HBCU (Historically Black College & University), you can safely assume that I like to wear nice gear and ride in a clean whip. But here is one hack that even you can use to this day.

In most cases, buying a brand-new car is a bad idea. Why? Because a vehicle depreciates by thousands of dollars right when you drive it off the lot. I will use a few of my past purchases as a baseline for you.

Example 1: I purchased a 2014 Mercedes-Benz E-Class two years after it hit the scene. This amounted to nearly $20,000 in savings. To take it one step further, I paid full price (all

$32,000) to avoid excess interest that car companies live for. The car was in phenomenal condition with only 26,000 miles and I saved tens of thousands of dollars.
Example 2: I bought my current 2022 5-series BMW new. I know what you are thinking, "Fletcher, you *just* said buying a brand-new car is a bad idea!" Hear me out though because this is one of the instances where it isn't necessarily. I purchased the car in Germany *where the brand originated.* I saved nearly $10,000 from the stateside sticker-price. And once again, I purchased it in-full avoiding any additional interest companies like to charge with monthly payments.

Did I need brand new cars? Absolutely not. But I have always been very satisfied with military life for affording me the opportunity to live the life I have dreamed of. Still, I remain humble and have always had mixed feelings mentioning my salary in this autobiography because I feel I may have been *somewhat* overpaid. But I feel like there will be plenty of opportunities to pay things forward starting with transparency on how I made it happen. Whether you make a lot or a little, it starts with your spending habits. Don't let the cars fool you. That is one of the only things I splurge on. The control and discipline I learned decades ago won't let me go beyond that.

I would be remised if I didn't say that I strongly feel senior NCOs are underpaid because they are the ones who make or break officers, do much of the officer's work, and have to balance their own work. They are held responsible for training our future leaders – both junior soldiers and junior officers. Nowadays, enlisted soldiers in today's military have as much (if not more) education as many officers. I feel junior enlisted soldiers make a fair salary because a 22-year-old E-4 or E-5 with only one or two years of college who makes $50,000 - $60,000 likely would not do much better in the civilian sector (after adding all the additional fringe benefits, of free health care, free housing, etc.). However, a 30 or 35-year-old E-6 or E-7, who only makes approximately $10-20K more than the E-4 or E-5, with a Bachelor's degree (and in some cases a Master's degree), is somewhat underpaid considering a 21-year-old Second Lieutenant with only a Bachelor's degree may make $15K more than the 35-year-old E-7. But that is a different fight for a different book.

CHANGE OF PLANS (2022-Now)

I was eligible to retire in January 2012, with 20 years of Active Federal Service (and let's not forget the little nest egg of four extra years of enlisted National Guard service). I was only 41 years old and thinking to myself just how easy it would be to start a second career if I wanted at that time. To be candid, my plan was always to retire immediately after reaching 20 years without doing a minute over. I never intended nor desired to achieve the rank of (full-bird) Colonel. The rank of Brigadier General wasn't anywhere in my vocabulary. The reason you ask? I always looked at things from a logical and monetary point of view. I always told myself I would lose money by retiring above the rank of Lieutenant Colonel. Obviously, that sounds ridiculous at first thought, but let me explain. Retiring as a Colonel or higher meant waiting for the additional time required for a promotion opportunity. During the wait, you must serve a three-year assignment at the rank to retire at that level. Anything less results in reverting back to a previous rank for retirement purposes. If I had retired from the military, at the 20-year mark, and started a brand-new job as a civilian, I would have received 50% of my Lieutenant Colonel salary from the military (the rank I held at the

20-year mark) and 100% of the salary from whatever civilian job I began at that 20-year mark. Committing to the next rank meant dedicating *more* time and initially sacrificing *more* money to fully reap the benefits.

So, there I was at a crossroads in January 2012 contemplating what would be best for me and my family. But I never would have thought that as I reached and surpassed the 20-year mark that I would continue to enjoy wearing the uniform and serving. It was as if I loved the job more than I did in the first half of my career. Up until the end, I continued to feel relatively young, full of energy, and my career was doing very well with the completion of two battalion level commands, two brigade level commands, Senior Service College/War College, and three GO level positions. It just may have been that passion showing through that lit my career up. Not to mention, several new variables came into play in my decision-making process over the recent years causing me to pass-up on the early retirement. Those include:

1.) Strong promotion potential to Colonel

Arguably the largest consideration was the fact that my career began to rocket after I became a Major. As a young Lieutenant and Captain, I would have never guessed that I would have been in such a strong and positive position in my career. After the Army began virtually trying its hardest to hand me a promotion on a silver platter, it became much harder to walk away from it. My hard work over the past decade of earning such great evaluation reports started to pay off. I have been fortunate enough to be selected for and completed: resident Senior Service College, two separate resident Master's degree programs, a battalion command equivalent position in my functional area as a Force Management Division Chief, a traditional battalion command in my basic branch of logistics, the opportunity to work with Congress in a leadership position, and being selected for and successfully completing brigade command while in a war-zone with outstanding Officer Evaluation Reports (OERs). I do not intend to be arrogant, but those accomplishments usually mean a promotion is destined.

2.) Responsibility to those living vicariously through me

The truth of the matter is that there are a lot of family members, distant relatives, friends, neighbors, and old church members from my younger years who were rooting me on to climb as high as I could. Many of my older friends and relatives with military experience served during the Vietnam era when racism was more prevalent. Since that era, we have seen many black officers achieve great success in the military. But my relatives and old neighborhood friends, most of whom have traveled very little from the impoverished conditions in which we were raised, do not know any black senior officers. To those friends and family members who rarely, if ever, travel outside a 50-mile radius of their northern Virginia neighborhood, "I am their Colin Powell." I could have literally *not* gotten promoted past the rank of Captain and they would have continued to hold me in very high esteem for achieving such high heights considering where my *starting line* was in life. In many ways, I felt a sense of responsibility to them to continue to be an example to them and their children. Although they may be surrounded by drugs and all types of illegal activity in their neighborhood, they still have an opportunity to escape the rat race they are currently in and pursue a different path. It may take a change to get better results.

3.) The "what if" factor

The burning question of "how far can I actually go" is another small variable that factored into my decision to continue the ride. This plays somewhat into the other two factors mentioned. It is ironic that a poor kid with a slight stutter back in the day (more noticeable in my youth, but only slightly noticeable today) would go on to become a General Officer by 46. It is comical that as one of eight children of a drunken father and a mother who raised us on welfare, neither of whom even went beyond the 10th grade, became a self-made millionaire by 43 and multi-millionaire at 48. With everything going against me, you have to wonder "how far can a broke kid like that go?" When looking through a photo album of my early childhood days of those dire and impoverished conditions, it is very easy for me to get inspired and motivated. Those memories help me to reach deep down, when needed, to tap into some intestinal fortitude to find the energy to continue to run faster and farther away from that *starting line* in life from which I started.

Here is where things get interesting. After 20-years of active duty, you qualify to receive 50% of your Base Pay in retirement. Not to mention there is an additional 2.5% added year over year. I retired on 31 May 2022 completing a total of 34 years and three months of total service. Of this service time, 29 years, seven months, and 10 days were spent on active duty when combining my Regular Army, AGR, and IMA time. This means that I was entitled to 74% of the average of my highest 36 months of Base Pay. Even though I lose out on BAS, BAH, and COLA, I can't complain with the passive income flow that's been created. Since we are all friends here now, I can tell you that the average Base Pay in this equation amounts to $13,812.20 leaving me with a whopping $10,221 that I began receiving, for military retirement, in May 2022, and the first of every month thereafter just for waking up and walking to the mailbox. Shout out to the Department of Defense for ensuring my check *always* arrives on time; with modern technology, it's actually direct-deposited into my account, but "waking up and walking to the mailbox" has a funnier ring to it. It doesn't hurt to add that these same monthly retirement checks increase annually with inflation. Get this. From 2022 to 2023, due to inflation, my military retirement increased from $10,221 for the month of December 2022 to the new and permanent amount of $10,670 for the month of January 2023 (and beyond, until the next inflation-increase in January 2024, and every year thereafter). Since I retired mid-year (May 2022, not January 1, 2022), I only received a portion of the 8.7% inflation increase received for the year 2023.

In addition to a monthly military retirement check of $10,670, I also receive an additional disability check from the Department of Veteran's Affairs (VA). My VA rating is 100% which means I also receive a separate and additional monthly check for $3,823.89 (which includes the 8.7% inflation increase for 2023). It is not uncommon for someone who spent 20-plus years in the military to receive a high rating from the VA. Sleep apnea alone was 50% and after wearing combat boots with little to no arch supports, sit-ups on concrete, and lots of running that involves excessive pounding on the knees and back, many veterans have pain in their back, hips, and knees. Some veterans can qualify for much higher amounts for the more serious issues where they may be confined to a wheelchair or severely impaired due to their service-connected disabilities. It is important to note that VA compensation is tax free and also increases annually with inflation. By law, monthly military pension payments (from the Department of Defense) and monthly VA disability compensation payments (from the Department of Veterans Affairs) are required to use the same Social Security Administration (SSA) calculation to keep benefits in line with rising prices. Since the SSA COLA increase, for 2023 was 8.7%, the DOD for military pensions and VA for disability compensation payments also increased by 8.7%.

My investments—mutual funds, index funds and ETFs combined—have grown to a principle of slightly higher than $3 Million (remember I said the 1st million was realized at age 43, and based on the 'Rule of 72,' which I'll discuss later, it doubles every 5-7 years, on its own, without me doing anything). The S&P 500 index has averaged annualized returns above 11% (11.88% to be exact) since adopting 500 stocks into the index in 1957. Some years, (particularly during a recession) the market may only average 1-3% or less, into the negatives, while there will be other years where they average well above 20%. Given the fact the stock market has averaged almost12% since its inception, even with all the wars, natural disasters, housing crash, auto industry crash, COVID, etc., it is fairly safe to assume it will continue to average close to this same % in the future. Therefore, it should also be safe to assume that my investments will earn, on average, $360,000 ($3,000,000 x 12% = $360,000) in dividends and capital gains without me ever touching the principal. It is a beautiful thing if you do not touch those dividends and capital gains (i.e., the interest made) and simply allow them to be reinvested into the principal. This is called *compounded interest* and means my $3,000,000 in principle will potentially earn $360,000 in dividends and capital gains bringing the total investment to $3,360,000 next year. If reinvested the following year, this nest egg will net $403,200 ($3,360,000 x 12% = $403,200) in dividends and capital gains bringing the total nest egg to $3,763,200 ($3,360,000 + $403,200 = $3,763,200) after two years and to $4,214,784 after three years and so on and so forth. If you never touch the interest earned and allow it to be added back to the principal, the base-line principal will continue to grow *by itself* without you doing anything. So, I believe I will land firmly on my feet if I continue following the saying made popular by Rapper 'Pit-Bull' and the renowned public speaker, Les Brown: "Shoot for the moon. Even if you miss, you will land among the stars." This quote simply assures me that even if I were to never make another profit from my investments again that I will *still* be just fine.

I can honestly say that my investments have tracked along in this positive manner for me thus far. My initial plan when converting from AGR to TPU, in order to accept my promotion to Brigadier General, was to simply stop reinvesting my dividends and capital gains and to live off of the interest earned without ever touching the principle. But fortunately, I was always able to serve enough days of active duty throughout the year where I have never had to touch either the principle or interest, allowing me to continue reinvesting all interest earned, thereby earning compounded interest. Isn't compound interest a dream?

So, let's break this (and more) down:

1.) Military Retirement of **$10,670 per month**. (O7/Brigadier General with over 34 years total service for pay purposes of which 29 years, 7 months, and 10 days being active duty). As noted, this is the amount for 2023 and increases annually with inflation. *(This amount is currently being received).*

2.) VA Disability of **$3,823.89 per month**. As noted, this also increases annually with inflation and this compensation is tax free. *(This amount is currently being received).*

3.) Rhonda's Civil Service Retirement of approximately **$2,500 per month**. A government/FERS retirement annuity benefit is based on a calculation of: Salary (average of highest 36 months; her salary was approximately $140,000), multiplied by .01, multiplied by the number of years of service completed, divided by 12 months, to equal a monthly civil service retirement. (Additionally, each year of inflation will also need to be added up until the year she begins collecting at 60). Her TSP was included in investments *(she could elect to begin receiving this civil service retirement at 57 1/2 but would incur a penalty because she is under 60, therefore since we do not need the money, she has deferred this monthly retirement benefit until she turns 60 to avoid the penalty – this is called a "deferred retirement").*

4.) Mutual Fund and TSP Disbursements would be approximately **$30,000 per month** assuming a 12% average rate of return will yield $360K per year. With the amount of my monthly military retirement and monthly VA compensation satisfying all my financial needs for now, I will continue to forgo tapping into these investments and will allow the profits to continue multiplying under the 'compounding' concept and the 'rule of 72'.

5.) Social Security *Projection* would be a collective **$9,386 per month** between Rhonda and I starting at age 70. You are allowed to designate when you receive social security. Fun fact, the longer you wait (up until age 70), the larger percent you receive. If you can defer, it always helps. Even though we are still a decade away from collecting social security, I wanted to set this in as a buffer. Social security may look different in the future, but it won't just disappear overnight.

This totals over $56,000 per month. It does not account for military retirement income or VA disability income increasing annually with inflation. It also does not account for investments continuing to multiply every year through the act of reinvestment. By simply letting the compound effect take place, my current $3,000,000 theoretically will become $24,000,000 in 21 years. This is known as the '*rule of 72*' where you double the base amount invested every seven years. See how I'm doing in 2043. Theoretically, based on the 'rule of 72' $3,000,000 in 2022 should double to $6,000,000 seven years later in 2029 if the stock market continues to average 12%. Seven years later in 2036, this $6,000,000 should double to $12,000,000, and double again from $12,000,000 to $24,000,000 in 2043. This of course is assuming you never touch the principle and continue to allow the interest earned and capital gains to be reinvested back into the principle without touching it (which is called *compounded interest)*. Keep in mind that I will continue to pay approximately one third of my income in federal taxes annually. Also know that the value I referenced is not guaranteed. *Defined-benefit plans* are the things I can count on (i.e., guaranteed) without them changing due to market conditions (i.e., military retirement, VA disability, Rhonda's civil service retirement, possibly Social Security providing it's still there). *Defined-contribution plans* on the other hand (specifically the mutual funds, index funds, ETFs, and TSP disbursements) are at their core investment accounts and mimic motions of the market itself.

Here's a quick tip regarding defined-contribution plans. Which means they have the potential of netting larger returns, but not 100% guaranteed. Fortunately, much of our investments are in government TSP accounts and Roth IRAs which are more secure. However, I am well diversified which means investments are split between various accounts including TSPs and Roth IRAs as mentioned, as well as several other non-Roth IRA *mutual fund, index fund and ETF accounts. There is always the rare chance that these non-Roth IRA accounts can yield very low returns during bear-market years. But as noted above, the stock market has averaged 12% from strong respected funds since the inception of the stock market, so it is safe to say that if a fund from a strong fund returns 1-3% in a bear-market, then it will very soon yield approximately 20% or higher in the bull-markets. This is because it will likely continue to average close to 12% over the life of the fund. Therefore, this $30,000 per month in investment income is simply an estimate if I were to begin receiving payment from the accounts today, but potentially a much larger amount the longer I wait to tap into it.*

After running the numbers, it was easy to finally answer the question: "when to retire?". I am 100% certain that if I were to begin receiving all that I am entitled to now, that I would not be able to spend it all. Additionally, I don't foresee making vast and drastic lifestyle changes in retirement where I begin spending double and triple what I currently spend. Therefore, since I am not currently spending all the monthly military retirement and monthly VA compensation, and we have yet to even begin receiving Rhonda's retirement, or social security, or tapping into investments, then what would the real purpose be to continue working? Sure, having served as a General Officer I'm sure I could draw up a nice-looking resume to land a nice high-paying executive level position. This type of job (or rather 'profession' at this level) causes you to remain in the 'rat race,' where you make a lot of money, but requires you to possibly live in an area that's not your dream retirement location and where you leave home when still dark, work all day, and return home when it's dark again. Although I was always dedicated to whatever profession I performed, whether as a soldier, security guard, newspaper employee, restaurant worker, etc., I never had the love or passion to do it for free. Sure, I would make a killing, but I'd never spend it. If I died today, I'd be leaving my son millions (that's plural with an "s"). And he doesn't need it either, because he has a steady income, he pins on the rank of Captain in May 2023, and he's already on a strong investment track himself. He invests $300 per month with the same company I started with as a young Lieutenant, Fidelity; and he also contributes another $400 per month into his TSP account, for a total of $700 per month. So, although I will definitely leave him all I have, he will become a millionaire on his own without me, in the same manner I did by contributing monthly to mutual funds, index funds, ETFs, and a TSP account. Therefore, continuing to work would cause me to earn more money than I need, causing me to pay even more in taxes, and causing me to only delay enjoying retirement. But I am very blessed to say this is a nice problem to have. This is what we say about taxes: we hate paying taxes, but it is a nice problem to have because it ultimately means we are making money.

I always thought I would likely pursue a career in the federal government as either a contractor or civil servant like Rhonda, when I retired from the military. With approximately 30 years of active-duty military service, reaching the rank of General Officer, a Top-Secret security clearance, two Master's degrees, as well as being a War College graduate, I am sure there are many (government) contract agencies that would be quick to offer big bucks for my services. That's not even considering the myriad of leadership positions to list on my resume. From leadership in Battalion Command, Brigade Command, Garrison Command, to strategic level experiences working in the Pentagon and with Congress, to two different four-star Combatant Commands, I've reached a point where the value I bring can only be matched by a select few. Although I loved serving in the Army, I am eager to dive into my next chapter. Don't get me wrong. I will miss the people, traveling for free, and of course the money, but I am not upset with the lifestyle we've managed to create. So far it entails waking up when the sun comes up, exercising, then killing time the remainder of the day with the television or on the computer researching information as we transition to being expats in Panama. With the country visa (i.e., residency) process behind us, life is more than good.

As far as money is concerned, it may seem like I make a lot of it and have a lot of it, but a wise man once said, "You will never get rich in the military, but at least you will never have to stand in the welfare line." I was actually this "wise" man many years ago who said and truly believed this statement. Needless to say, it can be very misleading. I have served my entire adult life in the military and considering how I have outlined how I have become a multi-millionaire; I believe I have proven that you can become rich in the military. Although the military alone did not make me rich, my wise decision to begin investing early as a young Second Lieutenant and to increase that monthly investment with each promotion and my discipline to stick with my investment plan long-term is what made me financially successful. But the military certainly provided a stable means and a comfortable paycheck that enabled me to make the financial decisions I made over the years. As a matter of fact, the second part about never having to stand in the welfare line if you are in the military is also false. I have read several articles in the paper where lower enlisted soldiers receive welfare to make ends meet. The only way to avoid this shortfall is to not live above your means and to set goals for yourself.

Maybe just maybe I will continue to push the envelope in retirement. I may consider serving on the Board of Directors for public and/or private companies. In late 2021, approximately six months prior to my retirement, a head-hunter organization reached out to me and explained that many corporations are attempting to diversify their boards to make them look more like America – as most boards currently consist of 'older white men.' As a black General Officer, they explained they could assist me in becoming a board member if I were interested. They sponsored me and paid for me to become Board Director certified through the American College of Corporate Directors (ACCD) by paying the $5,000 fee for my four-month training. They also assist in finding board opportunities and they collect a finder's fee (from the company that hires me, not from me).

The average pay for Board of Directors positions is approximately $30,000 a year and can go up much higher for more well-known companies. There is usually an extra $10,000 for each committee you serve on as well. As a former military General, I would be well suited for the committee that sets strategic policy and strategic direction for the company or hires and fires C-Suite leadership (i.e., the company president, VP, CEO, COO, CFO, etc.). Most Board Members who do this type of work serve on a few boards simultaneously across different companies along with one or two committees for each board. The work (on average) consists of attending one in-person meeting a quarter and usually one zoom conference a week. Therefore, if you sit on the Board of Directors for two different companies and belong to two committees with each board, you will likely earn approximately $100,000 annually (2x boards at $30,000 each + 4x committees at $10,000 each). That kind of cash paired with a big fancy title of "Member of the Board of Directors" is certainly a nice gig to have for such little work involved (of approximately one in-person meeting per quarter and one zoom meeting per week). I am still interested in this opportunity, not so much for the money, but to keep busy; but our decision to become expats in Panama has placed this option on the back burner. Regardless of if I decide to pursue a board seat or not, I remain board certified through ACCD, and will always have that as an option depending on where exactly I end up.

I WISH (Now)

Skee-Lo had it all wrong back in 1994. He wished for height, athleticism, affection, and a '64 Impala. But if he had just wished for financial literacy, he could have had all of that and so much more.

By not teaching a timely and relevant curriculum around financial aptitude, our school system is unwittingly condoning our poor and reckless societal norms of "keeping up with the Jones'," a completely different life game so many are currently playing. Society would lead us to believe, especially for a young kid in grade school, that having the latest Nike Air Jordans is the coolest thing and to buy them on the first day they are released when they cost the most. I admit, in many ways I too am susceptible to this mindset of spending more than necessary. I drive a brand new 5-series BMW and prior to this vehicle I drove a nearly new E-class Mercedes Benz. And my wife drives a Land Rover Range Rover Sport (that she bought new on her own from her earnings). Although we can easily afford it, I would have definitely been better served by buying a Toyota Corolla for myself and a Toyota Rav4 for my wife. Why a Toyota Corolla you ask? In the 1996 book *The Millionaire Next Door* written by Thomas Stanley and William Danko, it is stated that the "average millionaire" drives a Toyota Corolla. You don't even know they're millionaires because they live so far below their means. In our defense, our vehicles are completely paid in full.

Going back to my comments of having so many useless bits of knowledge, from grade school, etched in our mind that will never be used, we all would be so much better served if we learned about financial acumen in grade school. Just picture this: You walk into an introductory course in elementary school with a topic written boldly on the board. "How to manage and balance a bank account." The class is filled with fun examples leveraging the math and reading skills you have built up over the years to interpret the numbers and notes that you see. Then, as you transition to middle school, you find a piece of paper on your desk as you walk into homeroom. You flip it over to find a list:

A. The importance of living below your means
B. What actually happens when bills aren't paid on-time
C. How to maintain a good credit score

You are then given the option to start with whatever subject you choose in a breakout session to learn more. Talk about a strong intermediate level. Finally, you find yourself preparing to graduate high school and move on into the real world. But before you leave, you have to research and prepare a "dissertation" on one of the following questions:

1. What does it mean to pay yourself first?
2. How would you create passive income if given $1,000?
3. What is 'compounded interest' and how does this multiply your money much faster in the stock market than an APR does with your savings account?
4. How would you explain the 'Rule of 72' or 'Dollar Cost Averaging' to a first grader?

With any of these questions answered, the student will be more prepared to take on the world than ever before. An advanced level of thinking will challenge them to challenge everything that they do.

Teaching financial literacy at the grade school level would no doubt lead to more adults making much better choices with their finances earlier in life. And when it comes to accumulating wealth, the earlier you start the better! I will just give this one example of how easy it is to accumulate a One-Million-Dollar nest-egg, on a middle-income salary. If someone earns a gross salary of $60,000 per year, their net pay (after taxes) will likely be approximately $49,442. If they live on only 80% of this net salary ($39,553) and invest the other 20% ($9,888) in an index fund averaging a 10% annual return, they will have:

$566,335 in 20 years
$1,626,516 in 30 years
$4,376,355 in 40 years

The only negative I see with this example is that we may very well see later on that $1,000,000 is not enough to retire on. It will be important to carve out even more than the 20% suggested before. Keep in mind this can also look like generating more income whether through your job(s) or passively.

Investing and money management in general is not complicated. In-fact, investing is very easy in theory, but it is extremely hard in practice, namely because most don't have the patience to stick with their plan for the long-term. They stop their investments when they don't see quick results. There is no single formula for achieving financial success, and there is no one-size-fits all approach. While it is very true that what works for one may not work for another, I do believe that successful investors—those who reach financial freedom—share similar traits:

1. they treat investing as a top priority, on par with the most essential bills in their budget,
2. they are willing to make short-term sacrifices for long-term gains,

3. and they practice the patience and discipline to stay the course with their investment over the long-term even if the market dips. In-fact, when the market dips, they do not cut and run, they view it as an opportunity to invest even more because they understand that the market will eventually rise again and will rise even higher than before, so essentially when the market dips, it means they are taking advantage of buying the same shares 'on sale,' because when the market recovers, they will have purchased those same shares at a discounted price.

In my opinion, there are three main ways to generate real wealth:
Take note; this may be one of the most important messages relayed in this book

1. investing in the stock market, whether through mutual funds, index funds or ETFs,
2. buying or building a business,
3. or investing in real estate.

I'm sure some have become wealthy in other ways (not counting winning the lotto or having a super talent in professional athletics or the entertainment industry), and there may even be one or two who became wealthy through a get-rich-quick scheme overnight, I just haven't seen any. The ultimate test for any wealth builder is to see if they managed to keep it without losing it just as fast as they won it. Just let those three methods listed above sink in.

To become wealthy, the business angle may be the most interesting because that is where you find the wealthiest people in the world. When you google "Forbes top 10 richest people in the world", you will find that all 10 made their wealth by either buying, building, or managing big businesses. If you were to ask the younger crowd, you would hear how they are finding new ways to create passive income every single day – their new-age form of creating a business. Whether it is creating computer and cellphone apps or building a community through content creation, people are getting more and more creative. Sure. Stocks and real estate will continue to be around for the foreseeable future, and make your financial dreams come true if you have the discipline to start early and live beneath your means. But don't be afraid to be creative!

Real estate, like business, can also provide huge wealth. It also provides great tax benefits (or rather great tax loopholes) which come in handy when you have millions to your name. You have the ability to make thousands in capital gains and dividends annually and have the choice to either freely give Uncle Sam a large portion or use the many 'legal' tax advantages that real estate offers. Average people who don't have businesses and real estate just don't have the same leverage.

Both the real estate and business methods to creating wealth do, however, require you to roll up your sleeves and put in the work required. The rewards are huge, but they are not something that you can put on auto-pilot and forget about. They require your time, oversight, and effort. The stock market option to gaining wealth is far less sexy than both the business and real estate options. In fact, if you're doing it right, it's extremely boring and that's exactly how it should be. Long-term investing is supposed to be boring. There's no exciting trick that will suddenly turn you into a millionaire overnight or in one month or even in one year; otherwise, everyone else would have already beat you to it. The only trick, if you can call it one, is to invest long-term regardless if the market is high or low and to increase your monthly contributions when possible.

The biggest factor with long-term investing is having the good fortune to start as early as possible to take advantage of compounding, which has the most significant impact on the growth of your investments. Here's a quick calculation to explain how compound interest works that any calculator will show: if you invest $1,000 per month at only an 8% return, which is very easy to get in the market, it would take 6.5 years to reach $100,000. It would then take only 4 more years to reach $200,000. And then only 3 years to reach $300,000. Notice how each $100,000 milestone is reached in a shorter period even though you're contributing the same amount monthly – that's the beauty of compound interest (and notice we used a much safer return of only 8%, even though the market has averaged almost 12% since its inception). Also, investing in the stock market is easier than ever. It no longer requires huge amounts of time following and researching individual stocks or managing portfolios. This type of investing is so boring because your one investment (and its best if you have more than one if possible) is pooled with other investors and being invested into multiple different companies that make up the 500 leading companies in the US (the S&P 500) such as Amazon, Apple, Exxon, Google, Microsoft, Tesla, just to name a few. Your only requirement is to make your monthly contribution and the fund manager does the rest.

On one hand, you could call this the perfect method for the "lazy investor." But since the stock market has returned almost a 12% average (11.88% to be exact) since its inception in 1957, it's probably not fair to say it's for the "lazy investor," but rather for the "smart investor." In all seriousness, if you have a full-time job, or simply have a busy life with little extra time, then buying or building a business and investing in real estate may be a bridge too far. Investing in the stock market, through mutual funds, index funds, and ETFs, however, may be the perfect option for you of the three discussed. Ideally, the most well diversified portfolio should have all three, but since the stock market is the easiest (or least time consuming) and requires less capital up front, then this method should definitely be included in your investment portfolio.

While mutual funds and index funds may not make you "private jet ownership rich" like owning a very successful business can, it can make you rich enough to qualify to be in the top 10%. That only requires having a net worth of $1.2 million. According to Investopedia, and several other financial sources, "the minimum net worth of the top 1% of households is roughly $11.1 million and the top 10% have a net worth of about $1.2 million." But the real goal with regard to wealth should not be an attempt to attain a certain dollar amount. Wealth should be an aim to attain a certain level of 'financial freedom.' This form of 'true wealth' (or financial freedom), is having complete control over your time and the freedom to choose how you spend it. Many confuse wealth with having expensive material possessions such as expensive cars, boats, planes, designer clothes, and large houses. These are actually debts and liabilities, and in some cases depreciable assets. Even houses could be a liability if they have no equity. Instead of expensive material possessions, real wealth allows you to live a healthy and joyful life by providing the freedom to do what you want when you want. Simply put, freedom should be your goal, not money; if you are disciplined with your investing and not trying to time the market, then the money will follow.

As I look back on my time in grade school, I think of just how much time was wasted. Although I did not receive this important financial awareness through any of my mainstream education programs, I was fortunate to have received it by working consistently since the age of 11. There is a popular saying that "hindsight is 20/20," and that is most true with money. As I reflect on my youth working and making money, I now see how beneficial those lessons were that I learned in financial management and fiscal discipline. Obviously, I made some poor choices with money as a pre-teen back in the day. But it was those experiences that gave me the opportunity to learn when I wasn't making a lot of money. Even though I made only a few hundred dollars a month in middle and high school, I would purchase a more expensive bicycle than I needed or buy two mopeds when I only needed one. But the lessons I learned in my teens by wasting $20 here or $100 there worked the same for me as the adult who wastes $5,000 or $10,000 just to learn the same lesson. This magnitude of loss causes the average Joe to delay, or never start, investing in their future or for their retirement. I managed to focus my attention on acquiring discipline and good work skills instead. News flash: mistakes are inevitable.

It is only a matter of how early you get to experience them to truly reap the benefits. Mistakes may linger, but they won't follow you if you make a point to learn from them. If you do not learn these important lessons early, these poor money choices can have life-altering consequences down the road that prevent you from paying yourself first.

I want to be very clear that this is in no way meant to be bragging or boasting but rather a *blueprint*. Simply put, I enjoy talking about money almost as much as I like watching it grow. Take this extensive deep dive as proof of my claim to being a multi-millionaire. Believe me when I say that some of my peers that also retired from the military in a myriad of different ranks cannot say the same and may even go to the extent to 'call BS.' Consider this tactical list of receipts as a reason on how it just might work for you in one way, shape or form. All you need is a little financial discipline to stick with a proven investment over a consistent period of time and allow the principles and theories of *dollar cost averaging* and *compounding* to work in your favor while the *rule of 72* does the rest. You'll surprise yourself with the result when you roll up your sleeves, put in the work, treat others with respect, and keep a positive outlook on life. I am a testimony to just how much it pays off. I challenge you to take what you need from this section. I believe the *blueprint*, from this small section, is worthy of being a stand-alone Children's Book, into finance for kids and those eager to learn more about money management.

PART IV – THE HANDOFF

I stepped up to the podium. Dimmed lights illuminated my audience as I looked from my right to my left. My gaze stopped as I saw a familiar face. He didn't seem surprised at all. After all we had been through, this was just another day for him. "Good morning! I hope you guys are as excited as I am because I am super excited for each and every one of you. You are about to become part of the MOST respected organization in the entire country. Don't take my word for it…", I continued speaking during the commissioning ceremony. Who would have thought that they would allow me to commission these graduates into Second Lieutenants? And even more, my son was right there on the front row, receiving his commission by me, his dad! "He finally made it," I thought to myself as I continued along with my prepared speech.

This was the proudest moment in my life. It wasn't just that my son had graduated college. It wasn't that he listened to every word I had said – at least the important ones. No, not at all. He did everything right and more. He was a student of the practice and constantly prioritized learning. He maintained an energy about him where he always expected more. He was on the edge of his figurative seat hungry for whatever knowledge I was willing to give him. He was ready for the ultimate handoff and his starting line was well ahead of the pack. His thriving existence has been validation in everything invested in him thus far. As a parent, you aren't just happy about their many accomplishments. You are happy when they are.

Closing out my 20 or so minutes of remarks… "I asked earlier, what type of officer do you want to be? Be the type who automatically treats everyone with dignity and respect at all times, and I guarantee you that your soldiers will appreciate you for it and they will make it their life's work to make your job as easy as possible and they'll ensure you succeed. So, without further ado, what do you say we make you Second Lieutenants!" The room was in an uproar.

My Son's Graduation and Commissioning Ceremony

FAMILY MATTERS (Now)

Steve Urkel may have been misunderstood back in the day. He was a constant nuisance to his neighbors, the Winslow's. His attachment to this close-knit family may have been because of tough acceptance from his own. Deep down, it was never about how much money he had, but how loved he felt. And you were reminded every time an episode aired that *Family Matters*.

I am a blessed man. I am an uncle to 19 nieces and nephews, and an additional 16 great-nieces and great-nephews. Obviously, I have great love for my family. I mean who doesn't? But the love that I have for my son, Fletcher, and my wife, Rhonda, is unmatched. To be candid, it was both of them who taught me how to love. My siblings and I were often shortchanged with affection. As much as our mother loved us, I don't remember her verbally saying she loved us. Maybe it was the fact that her father raised her. Maybe it was her simply saving her energy to just make it through to the next day. When growing up in the environment we did, you must have a certain type of *toughness* to make it through. That same toughness can callous over the love that you have to offer. All too many times, the people that we depended on growing up let us down time and time again. We were closed and cold simply because if we weren't, we would be taken advantage of. But love is a muscle, and in order to grow it, you must use it.

My wife can attest that I changed with the introduction of our son. We openly show him our love and he does the same. Steve Harvey tells a joke that his father never said, "I love you," but he knew that he did because he "came back home after work each day." This is a common mentality in an environment like the one where I grew up. It's not that there isn't enough time to say those three meaningful words and to express your feelings to one another, but rather that there are more important things to be concerned with. Many parents were worried about scraping by for their next meal, making their next dollar, and trying to live their life without being taken advantage of. You do not want to be the weakest link in your underprivileged environment because the weakest one is likely to be the first who will be eaten alive in the *real world.* To protect yourself from being eaten alive in that ecosystem, it is best to have a coat of armor around you. You must be hard and cold. It is tough to shield yourself from all the many pitfalls in an underprivileged environment. I've come to learn that every time you express your inner feelings, you let your guard down just a tad bit more, even if it means you are only telling someone close that you love them.

I can honestly say the best thing that has ever happened to me is not my multiple college degrees or military rank I have attained, but the simple fortune of being blessed with someone special that supports me and loves me unconditionally. Rhonda checks all the blocks: she believes in God and helped to instill that in our son, she is a great mother, she is educated, she works and contributes to the household, and something that is important to me is that after she is finished working, she does not have a problem with cooking dinner in the evening. Plus, she is pretty. The Virgo in me tries to balance her kindness best it can. I am very neat and orderly and don't mind cleaning up a little after the fact. I do not follow the horoscopes closely, but that attribute always sticks out when I periodically find them.

WONDER WOMAN (1993-2017)

Rhonda was fortunate enough to complete her Master's degree while in

Germany. She earned a Master's degree in Business Administration from the University of Maryland. Actually, we both started together sitting side by side for our first class. She went on to complete the Master's degree program there while I transferred and completed my Master's degree from Florida Tech (and my second Master's degree from National Defense University in conjunction with the Army War College). She began working as a government civil service employee in Germany in 1993. She started as an Education Technician in the Army Education Center and also worked as a Contract Specialist with the Contracting Command in Germany. Upon moving back to the states, she worked with the Department of Commerce and the Department of the Navy. While assigned to Fort Lee, she completed a '7-9-11' Intern program where she was a GS-11 Logistics Management Specialist with U.S. Army CASCOM, that ultimately aided her climb to GS-15 towards the latter part of her career. While assigned to Puerto Rico, she did not work a full-time position. She worked part-time as a substitute teacher, which is equivalent to part-time civil service work because the school was located on the military base and therefore falls under Department of Defense Education Activity (DoDEA). Upon our return to the States, she began working for the Institute of Heraldry at Fort Belvoir as a Quality Assurance Specialist. She then transferred to Marine Corps University at Quantico Marine Corps Base as an Instructional Systems Specialist. Next up, she transferred to the Department of Justice at the Federal Bureau of Investigation (FBI) as an Instructional Systems Specialist at the FBI Academy at Headquarters Quantico.

During my assignment in Hawaii while completing my Battalion Command assignment, Rhonda took a two-year leave of absence from civil service and from full-time employment to once again work as a substitute teacher for the state of Hawaii, and also to be a housewife and stay-at-home Mom. Every now and again, the school system would call and ask her to teach (as we had a very active son who played a sport every school quarter). Upon our return from Hawaii back to the northern Virginia area, she initially worked as a contractor instead of a civil service employee with the Central Intelligence Agency (CIA). She would have loved to have gotten another GS job as an Instructional Systems Specialist with any government agency in the area, but she stumbled across an opportunity which was simply too good to turn down. Her contract paid $109 per hour (1,925 hours per year) to do Instructional Systems Specialist work for CIA

University which basically means she was on a team that developed educational curriculum for the various courses taught at CIA University (the same thing she had done at the FBI Academy, Marine Corp University, and DOD school houses). She worked at CIA University for only two years, capitalizing on the huge payday of $109 per hour (which equaled approximately $210K per year) before converting back to civil service and taking a supervisor position with the FBI Academy at Quantico as a Supervisory Instructional Systems Specialist. She rose to the rank of 'Acting GS-15' in this position. A GS-15 is roughly equivalent to the military rank of Colonel. She took a break again, from civil service to accompany me during my last two-year assignment in Stuttgart, Germany. Upon our departure from Germany, she was able to secure a civil service position with Homeland Security, at a facility near the Georgia-Florida border, so we settled in Jacksonville, FL, while she completed her civil service career.

She completed a deferred retirement in November 2022, with 21 years and seven months of civil service. She was eligible to retire at the 20-year mark, but because she does not have 30 years of service or the 56 ½ year age requirement, she would take a penalty for each year she is below the age of 60. Since we do not need the money, she elected to in-fact retire, but simply forgo receiving a retirement check until age 60 to avoid any penalties. Her unfortunate breaks from full-time employment, during a few of our oversees tours, caused her to lose out on completing more years of service. But it also afforded her the opportunity to be a full-time stay at home mom to our son, which may have indirectly helped him to stay focused throughout key periods of his youth as we continued to move frequently from one military assignment to another. She would have much rather continued her government employment without a break in service, but unfortunately at the higher GS levels, it is much harder to bounce from one government job to the next with every military PCS move. There are many GS-5, GS-7, and GS-9 positions all over, but the job opportunities well above GS-12 and at the senior GS-14/15 levels are much harder to walk right into (typically those that require not only a four-year degree, but graduate level courses as well as previous supervisory experience). It is always much harder for a senior-level civilian-working-spouse during each military move.

LIKE FATHER, LIKE SON (2002-Now)

Would you believe that this entire work sparked from a college assignment years ago? Back in August of 1988 on my first day of class as a freshman at Norfolk State University, one professor tasked the class to write a bio in two pages or less. This bio was only meant for him to know a little more about members of the class. For whatever reason, I kept adding to that page every so often. Sometimes there would be breaks of months. Other times, there were breaks for years. Regardless of the length of the gap, I would dust off the pages, add a few paragraphs, and store it back in a safe place. But I continued with no real expectations. That was until Fletcher Valdez Washington II was born on March 27, 1997. This is something I take a small bit of credit for.

My wife and I have invested in our son and our investments show the fruits of our labor. We have invested time, love, and money in him. By money, I am referring to paying for private school tuition and taking him on vacations around the world regularly. We try to do a cruise annually. By the time he was 13, he had 10 cruises under his belt. And by the time he graduated from college, at age 22, he had well over 15 cruises under his belt. He would have had several more, but during his teen years when he was old enough and tired of cruises, he would often ask to stay with a friend or relative instead of cruising with Rhonda and me, because he was simply *cruised out*.

Being so well traveled relates to my son because if you recall earlier, I spoke of my belief that the SATs are biased and how the strategy for scoring high on the SAT and for successful college admission begins very early in a child's life. It involves intellectual stimulation from the cradle through preschool and through grade school which most African-Americans in the lower socio-economic percentiles do not receive. I spoke of how parents should encourage their child's growth by promoting reading at an early age, scheduling vacations around their child's interests to stretch their imaginations and make them think more broadly and deeply. Although my son grew tired of the extensive traveling during his youth, I am certain his exposure and overall awareness of the world in general was invaluable and helped prepare him immensely for not only the SAT, but for life in general.

By attending a private Christian School for his first few years of schooling, taking him to church with us on Sundays, as well as setting a good upstanding example for him daily, my son has developed a strong foundation with good Christian values. He is a fast learner all because my wife and I placed him in positions to learn. He began attending a private Christian school at age three as opposed to the normal babysitter and began reading at the age of four. He only attended the private Christian school his first two years, for pre-school and kindergarten, to instill good reading habits and good manners early on (also I noted that during his pre-school year, it was cheaper than a baby-sitter). He switched to public school for elementary, but he was already well ahead on the reading level by then. He has always been very active in all of the Youth Sports Activities both on the military base and off through local community leagues whether basketball, football, t-ball, or soccer. We routinely sent him to either the Washington Redskins' Football Camp or Baltimore Ravens' Football Camp every summer and only stopped after he transitioned into varsity football which required participation, conditioning, and training during the summer months. Incidentally, I attended his summer camps with the Redskins and Ravens and served as a Counselor at the camp.

My Son and I Attending the Pro Bowl in Hawaii

Fletcher even followed my interest in Martial Arts. I earned a yellow belt in Taekwondo. It just so happens that my son also practiced karate and loved it. He attained a green belt in Taekwondo before we moved to Puerto Rico. We were just unable to find a Taekwondo dojo where the instruction was taught in English. We could only find Spanish speaking studios, so he had to reluctantly discontinue practicing karate. Obviously, as a young kid, he was not learning to fight. I simply enjoyed and appreciated the great deal of discipline and respect he learned from the classes.

He was actually the Class Valedictorian at his middle school graduation ceremony by scoring a perfect 4.0 GPA while simultaneously playing a sport every quarter, the true definition of a scholar athlete. He played the quarterback position and started all through his Middle School and High School years. He graduated from high school with a 3.75 GPA in all Honors and dual college credit classes. Aside from all of that, the fact that he is grounded, has a good heart, and believes in God are what I am most proud of about him. He graduated from the University of Tampa with a Bachelor's degree in communications after turning down the opportunity to play football as a quarterback for several universities. He saw the value in competing academically at the more well-known schools, versus competing athletically at a smaller D2 school. He eagerly wanted to play football as a quarterback at the collegiate level. He is truly my mini-me, with all my genes to boot – both the good and bad. Looking almost identical as me, standing at 5' 11" and weighing only 175 lbs. in his senior year, he received only offers from the smaller lesser known D2 schools, as the more well-known D1 schools want their quarterbacks to be in the 6'2" and above, and 220 lbs. and above range. It was his mature and wise decision to walk away from football and choose a school based on its education and not its athletics. He received an academic scholarship to attend the University of Tampa. In his first semester, he chose to enroll in Army ROTC as an elective because he had several dual college credits that transferred from high school. After the first year in ROTC, he won a full ROTC scholarship that covered tuition, fees, room and board. His scholarship also paid for his books and paid him a monthly stipend ($500 per month that went directly to his savings account for him to spend as he saw fit).

He found the time to play on the school's intramural flag football league and relive his quarterbacking dream. He managed to win the championship in his last two years satisfying his longing and love for the game. ROTC proved to be a great substitute for the physicality, teamwork, and comradery that being on a football team offered. With four years of ROTC under his belt, he managed to earn an Army commission as a Second Lieutenant with his Bachelor's degree just like me upon graduating. He is currently a 1st Lieutenant in the Army Transportation Corps (the same branch I was commissioned into) and completed assignments as Platoon Leader and G-3 Training Officer in the 82nd Airborne Division, at Fort Bragg, NC. He is currently assigned as a Company Executive Officer within the Sustainment Brigade of the 82nd Airborne Division. He'll

PCS to Ft Lee, VA, in March 2023 to attend the Advanced Course, and will pin Captain in May 2023, so he is well on his way doing great things.

Fletcher is truly *'his father's son'*. He looks like me, has the same name, has the same profession (an Army Transportation Officer), was fortunate to graduate from college debt-free, an Alpha-Man, *and* he managed to be just as financially savvy. Just as I began my large mutual fund investments as a young Second Lieutenant, he chose to do the same mutual fund investments with the same company I use shortly after he commissioned as a young Second Lieutenant as well. He started, as a Second Lieutenant contributing $300 per month to a Roth IRA mutual fund and $400 per month to his military TSP. In addition to his military insurance which is only term insurance that will cease when he exits the military, he has a separate *universal* life policy just like me (basically a *blended* policy that lasts forever and never increases like a whole life policy, but costs much less like a term policy). He plans to increase both his military TSP account and his Roth IRA mutual fund account with each promotion, just as I had done throughout my career. So, even without me leaving my nest egg to him (which I will absolutely do), he is definitely on his way to becoming financially independent on his own without my help.

The reason this book exists is because of my son. I started adding with the purpose of helping him understand some important things. Maybe, just maybe if I could recall my life journey one more time, then he would understand just the magnitude that I wanted him to succeed. I want him to know that he grew up with parents who love him, have multiple college degrees each, and worked professional careers. I want him to know that he taught me how to love openly and willingly. It's true that my son lacked very little while growing up. Compared to my childhood, he essentially grew up with a silver spoon in his mouth. I worried so much because some strengths and positive traits are best learned through experience, those same experiences that he had to go through on his own. Any parent will understand when I say it is a torturous struggle to want to give your child the world *especially* when you have the financial means to do so. But you want them also to acquire those morals, self-satisfaction, and other inner strengths that only come from rolling your sleeves up and working hard for it yourself. I am pleased to say he has learned the intangibles through an alternative means to hardship. He is humble, kind, successful and God-fearing. My level of pride is compounded considering my *starting line* that I have continued to highlight throughout this book. Hopefully, this book gives him a good understanding and appreciation of my childhood and helps him not to take life for granted. I dedicate this work to my only son, the greatest gift God has given my wife and I.

CONCLUSION

I began by posing the often quoted Million Dollar question that goes something like: "what is (or how do you attain) true happiness and success?" Although I am both fortunate and blessed to say I have achieved both, I have also learned that they are interdependent and mutually exclusive where one does not drive the other. My many successes in life, both professional and financial, do not drive my happiness. Being married to a beautiful God-fearing woman makes me happy. Seeing my son make good life decisions makes me happy. Trying to live a life where I give more than I receive not just financially, but through love, dignity, respect, and mentorship makes me happy. Lending a helping hand to subordinates, peers, friends, or even a complete stranger makes me happy.

I am often told by many how they are so proud of me for accomplishing all that I have, especially considering my *starting line* in life was pushed back a little farther than most. I have reached great heights thus far in life and still have energy in my body to stride even farther. In this autobiography, I relayed why many of my brothers and sisters and I have such a burning desire to run as far and as fast as we can away from our *starting line.* It would be selfish and arrogant to think that I achieved all my success alone. The kindness and respect that I have shared with so many over the years has been returned ten-fold and for that, I am forever grateful. I am a firm believer in God and give Him all the glory for my many successes. As Philippians 4, 13 says: "*I can do all things through Christ who strengthens me.*" As I reflect on my life, I am often reminded of the popular hymn that reads:

It reads:
"I Don't Feel No Ways Tired, I've Come Too Far From Where I Started From.
Nobody Told Me That The Road Would Be Easy.
I Don't Believe He Brought Me This Far To Leave Me."

Additionally, considering my strides thus far, I often reflect upon and identify with Marvin Sapp's popular Gospel song entitled *"I Made It."*

The lyrics are:

"Never Would Have Made It. Never Could Have Made It Without You.

I Would Have Lost It All. But Now I See How You Were There For Me.

I'm Stronger. I'm Wiser. I'm Better; So Much Better.

I Can Stand Here and Tell You;

I Made It!

I Made It!

I Made It!"

Thank you for reading my autobiography. I hope you have learned something, and I hope you will be a better person for it.

God Bless you and yours.

Warm Regards,
Fletcher

APPENDIX

PREVIOUS MILITARY ASSIGNMENTS

Note: This entire section is simply my duty descriptions from my different jobs held since being in the military and taken verbatim from my Officer Evaluation Reports (OERs).

My first duty assignment was as a **Platoon Leader** in Mannheim, Germany of 1st Platoon, 41st Transportation Company. Responsible for the health, welfare, morale, discipline, training, mission performance, and combat readiness of 43 soldiers and noncommissioned officers. Responsible for the daily operation and material readiness of 20 line-haul truck tractors, one High Mobility Multipurpose Wheeled Vehicle (HMMWV), and other organic equipment with a combined value in excess of $1.25 million. Additional duties included Company Executive Officer, Supply Officer, Unit Status Report Officer, Drug and Alcohol Officer, and Food Service Officer.

In my next assignment, I served as an **Operations Officer and Executive Officer** of the 15th Movement Control Team (MCT) in Frankfurt, Germany. Responsible for 23 soldiers, 29 Local National civilians, seven Branch Movement Control Teams, and a Rail Movement Management Team. Responsible for the management and coordination of all freight and container movement for the 1st Armored Division, 16th Corps Support Group, and V Corps units throughout a 25,000 square-mile region in central Germany. Primary manager for the maintenance of three tactical vehicles and over $375,000 of automation equipment. Additional duties included Supply Officer, Security Officer, and Unit Maintenance Officer.

I then served as a **Rear Detachment Commander** in Hanau, Germany of a Movement Control Team (MCT) that consisted of six Branch Movement Control Teams and a Rail Movement Management Team. Responsible for the training, preparation and deployment of all newly arriving soldiers in support of Operation Joint Endeavor. Responsible for providing both logistical and administrative support to the forward deployed MCT. Responsible for supporting all family members of the MCT by maintaining a strong Family Support Group and reacting to any and all requests, questions, concerns and needs of the family members. Responsible for the training, welfare and morale of five Rear Detachment soldiers; providing support for 44 deployed soldiers; and the supervisory oversight of 23 foreign national civilians.

I then served as an **Operations Officer and Movements Officer**, in Virginia Beach, VA, 11th Transportation Battalion (Terminal Service), Fort Story, VA, a multi-functional contingency force battalion, consisting of five companies and four detachments, with over 950 soldiers in 57 different jobs/specialties and 199 different pieces of equipment. Responsible for deliberate and contingency planning and coordination for reception, staging and onward movement terminal missions in support of a force projection Army. Planed for joint and single service missions including fixed port operations, logistics over the shore operations, amphibious movement of cargo and personnel, automated cargo documentation, lighterage control, harbormaster operations, water production/storage and fuel pipeline operations. Supervised and managed all aspects of the battalion's movements and operations in support of any worldwide contingency mission.

My "branch qualifying" (BQ) and "key & developmental (KD) job as a Captain was **Company Commander** in Virginia Beach, VA of a Headquarters Transportation Company (plus two Detachments all simultaneously), 11th Transportation Battalion (Terminal Service), Fort Story, VA consisting of 188 soldiers employed in the command and control of Terminal Operations (Fixed Port) and Logistics Over the Shore (LOTS) Operations. Responsible for developing and maintaining a deployable ready company, capable of accomplishing all its war-time and peace-time missions with short notice and the flexibility to support a wide range of operational contingencies throughout the entire battalion. Responsible for the training, supervision, welfare, safety, and families of all soldiers assigned to the unit. Responsible for maintaining over 1,500 end items of equipment valued in excess of $10 million and for maintaining several buildings, to include the troop living area and unit work area.

Upon completion of my Company Command position, I was selected to attend the **Logistics Executive Development Course – Florida Institute of Technology (LEDC-FIT)** in residency. This is the Army's most senior logistics course. It is a year-long course conducted through Florida Tech but held at Fort Lee, VA (the home of Army logistics) and awarded a Master's degree in Logistics Management, from Florida Tech.

I then served as a **Combat Developer and Force Integrator** in Petersburg, VA, U.S. Army Combined Arms Support Command (USACASCOM), Fort Lee, VA responsible for developing the force structure to enable the Transportation Corps to provide worldwide Force Projection and Theater distribution support. Analyzed doctrine, organizations and requirements to maintain an effective and viable Transportation Corps during Total Army Analysis. Responsibilities included, but was not limited to, leading and participating in studies, projects, conferences, and force development programs; coordinating with Department of the Army Staff, Major Commands (MACOMs), proponent schools and other integrating staff agencies regarding transportation force structure projects; preparing and presenting briefings to General Officers, Senior Executive

Service (SES) personnel, and USACASCOM representatives; and serving as the Transportation Corps representative and subject matter expert regarding Army Transformation.

During this tour at USACASCOM at Fort Lee, I also completed a six-month **deployment to Kuwait** where I served as **Deputy Chief of Air Operations** for the Forward deployed Coalition Forces Land Component Command (CFLCC) in support of Operation Enduring Freedom. Responsible for the planning and coordination of intra-theater airlift operations for an area of responsibility (AOR) consisting of 14 countries in support of the CFLCC mission to support United States Central Command. Interfaced with sister services and coalition forces from Germany, France, Canada, Great Britain, and Australia for the organization, implementation and the operational support of the entire Coalition Joint Operations Area (CJOA). Interfaced with transportation movement control organizations and mode operators to support reception, staging, and onward integration (RSOI) operations in the Central Command AOR.

I then served as an **Operations Officer** for the 166th Area Support Group (ASG) at Fort Buchanan, Puerto Rico responsible for the overall operations of the entire ASG, which consisted of three battalions (one Transportation, one Quartermaster, and one Maintenance Battalion) totaling 19 separate companies, of over 2,200 soldiers and civilians, spread throughout the entire island of Puerto Rico. I was the primary coordinator between the ASG and the 65th Regional Readiness Command's (its higher headquarters) Deputy Chief of Staff G3 Operations and other Staff elements and subordinate units for planning, developing, and direction readiness and operations of the ASG, to ensure the integration of the functions of supply and services, transportation, maintenance, aviation logistics, and medical service. I determined requirements and allocation of resources. I assisted subordinate unit commanders in improving readiness. I coordinated operational missions with 65th RRC for emergency operations and with U.S. Army South (USARSO) for humanitarian exercises and disaster relief operations.

During this assignment in the 166th ASG as the **Operations Officer**, my unit was **deployed to Baghdad, Iraq** for 12 months where the unit served as the Garrison Command Headquarters for the entire Victory Base Complex (VBC) located in Baghdad, Iraq. I was responsible for the planning and coordination of all Garrison Command Operations on the VBC to include: Camps Victory, Liberty, Slayer, Striker, Seitz, and Baghdad International Airport (BIAP). I was the primary coordinator between the ASG and the Multi-National Corps – Iraq (MNC-I) C3 and other Staff elements and subordinate units for the planning, developing, and directing readiness and operations, to ensure the integration of the functions of supply and services, transportation, engineering, base operations, and force protection for all tenant Coalition Forces in support of the Garrison Command's and Camp Mayor's mission success in the War on Terror.

Upon my return from Iraq, I transferred from the Area Support Group to its higher headquarters, the 65th Regional Readiness Command (RRC) where I served as the **Force Development Officer** for the RRC responsible for managing Force Structure and Modernization actions for a command of 48 units and over 5,500 authorized soldiers and civilians. Documenting and reviewing equipment resource requirements, authorizations and supporting plans. Responsible for maintaining MTOE/TDA documentation audit trails on all additions, deletions and other changes.

Serving as the command's Project Manager for all force modernization actions related to New Equipment Fielding and Training. Fund Manager for all Reserve Pay and Allowances (RPA) and Operations and Maintenance, Army Reserve (OMAR) allotments assigned to the Deputy Chief of Staff, Force Development (DCSFD). Reviewing and approving the orders associated with new equipment fielding and training. Reviewing, developing and supervising execution of manpower policy, plans, programs and procedures pertaining to TDA military and civilian actions, and supervising the Force Development Division Staff.

I then PCS'd from Fort Buchanan, Puerto Rico to the Office of the Chief, Army Reserve (OCAR) Force Programs Directorate where I served as a **Transportation Force Integrator and Organization Integrator** responsible for managing 100% of the Army Reserve's transportation units. Represent the Army Reserves at Headquarters Department of the Army, Department of Defense and the Joint Chiefs of Staff level on all transportation force structure, modernization and mobilization issues. Serve as the OCAR lead for transportation transformation. Conduct analysis of the current and projected transportation force and prepare options and recommendations for the Army Reserve during the Total Army Analysis, Quadrennial Defense Review, Functional Area Assessment, Command Plan Process and Force Design Updates. Maintain liaison with the Transportation School, Combined Arms Support Command, Major Army Commands and the Army Staff to ensure all actions and initiatives represent the Army Reserve in the most favorable manner and provide for a relevant and ready Army Reserve Transportation force.

Upon promotion to LTC, I was immediately selected, over more senior LTCs, to serve in a branch qualifying (battalion command equivalent) position for a LTC 50A/Force Management Officer as **Division Chief, Structure and Requirements Division** in the OCAR Full Time Support (FTS) Directorate responsible for the supervision of two Branches: the AGR Management Branch and the Data Management Branch, composed of seven Command Managers and Data Managers, both Military and civilian, executing the Chief, Army Reserves (CAR's) Title 10 functions. Responsible for the oversight of over 4,200 AGR authorizations above Troop Program Units to include Army Commands, Army Service Component Commands, Direct

Reporting Units, DA and DOD staffs as well as the Joint Staff. Manages the validation, reconciliation and execution of changes to AGR authorizations ensuring the CAR's priorities are met with maximum efficiency and focus. Conducts liaison and works with Army Commands and Agencies in providing guidance and assistance on manpower management issues. Manages the Directed Military Overstrength (DMO) program for the CAR.

Upon completion of my LTC branch qualifying position, I was selected to complete **Senior Service College (SSC)** in residency. I completed the Joint Advanced Warfighting School (JAWS) at the Joint Forces Staff College in Norfolk, VA. This is a Military Education Level-1 (MEL-1 or MEL-A) producing "Army War College" equivalent course and also awards a Master's degree in Joint Campaign Planning and Strategy, from National Defense University (this was my second Master's degree). Selection for and attendance at SSC is a huge accomplishment in an officer's career. SSC is the highest level of professional military education (PME) for an officer, with the exception of the short CAPSTONE course for Flag level officers (Generals, Admirals, and SES civilians). It is generally understood and believed that an LTC who gets selected for resident SSC has successfully completed a BQ/KD job as a LTC and will very likely get promoted to (full-bird) Colonel in the near future.

Upon completion of SSC in June 2010, I was selected, from a highly competitive board, to serve as a **Battalion Commander** of the Support Battalion, 196th Infantry Brigade, at Fort Shafter, HI. Responsible for providing quality training support to U.S. Army Reserve Component and National Guard combat arms, combat support and combat service support units throughout the Pacific Rim in order to enhance and maintain combat readiness and to develop, plan, coordinate and synchronize training support in accordance with the Army Force Generation (ARFORGEN) Training Model. Provide Mobilization Assistance Teams to assist in the mobilization training, certification and deployment of Army Reserve component units. Provide reinforcing support to 1st, 2nd, and 3rd battalions of the 196th Infantry Brigade.

This was my 2nd battalion level command. My previous assignment as a Division Chief on the OCAR staff qualified as a battalion command equivalent in my functional area of 50A/Force Management. Because I was fortunate enough to complete both that previous BQ assignment as well as SSC fairly early with several more years before I would be eligible to compete for promotion to O6, I took the opportunity to apply and compete for a traditional battalion command in my basic branch of logistics that carries the actual title of "Battalion Commander" that promotion boards understand without having to be briefed beforehand which battalion command equivalents qualify and do not qualify as BQ/KD assignments for LTCs. Additionally, although promotion board members are briefed beforehand of which additional jobs count as battalion command equivalents, it is my opinion that many of the "old school" senior officers who spent their entire careers in the "muddy boots" Army with soldiers (not civilians) may not respect the battalion command equivalents as much as the actual title of Battalion Commander. Fortunately, I was selected for an actual battalion command opportunity, so my file/record now shows that I have completed both a traditional battalion command in my basic branch as well as a battalion command equivalent in my functional area.

Upon completion of Battalion Command in June 2013, I was promoted from Lieutenant Colonel to full-bird Colonel and again selected, from a highly competitive board, to serve as a **Division Chief of the Congressional Operations Division** in the Office of the Chief of Legislative Liaison, in the Pentagon. Responsible for the synchronization of six separate Divisions all supporting the Chief, Legislative Liaison (CLL) to formulate, coordinate, supervise, and execute the Army's Congressional policy and strategy of building trust and confidence among Members of Congress and staff to broaden their understanding and advocacy of Army programs; oversees the OCLL's internal and external reporting, meetings, and processes; produces plans and orders to execute the CLL's intent; oversees Legislative Assistants to the Sergeant Major of the Army; manages the Congressional Fellowship program and Army Congressional Fellows; ensures Congressional trips maintain high legal and ethical standards; also serves as the CLL's Principal Advisor for Reserve Affairs to include both the National Guard and Army Reserve, ensuring both COMPOs support the CLL's and Senior Army Leadership's Total Army vision.

My tour in the Pentagon's Army Legislative Liaison Office was cut short after only six months because I was once again selected, from a highly competitive board, to serve, this time, as a **Brigade Commander** of the 647th Regional Support Brigade in El Paso, TX, at Fort Bliss. This was a two-year tour of command where the first year I was deployed to Kandahar, Afghanistan as a Garrison Commander and the second year I was "supposed" to be a traditional Brigade Commander responsible for the command and control of three Logistics Battalions throughout west-Texas and east-New Mexico, comprised of 1,300 soldiers and civilians. However, I was pulled from Brigade Command, upon my return from Afghanistan, to serve as the Rear Expeditionary Sustainment Command (ESC) Commander for the year that my boss was deployed to Kuwait – a 1-star General Officer job (that I'll highlight in the next paragraph). The job description for my **Garrison Commander** position was as follows: Responsible for commanding in a combined/joint environment in support of Operation Enduring Freedom, on the NATO Kandahar Airfield, Afghanistan. Directs, coordinates, supervises, and trains 50 Garrison Staff members that directly support 27,000 U.S. Armed Forces, Coalition Forces, DOD civilians, and contractors. Supports National Service Elements from Bulgaria, United Arab Emirates, Romania, Georgia, and Slovakia. Coordinates with Commander, Kandahar Airfield (COMKAF), Regional Command South (RC(S)), the theater

Expeditionary Sustainment Command (ESC), U.S. Forces Afghanistan (USFOR-A), and Coalition partner staffs. Engages multiple contract oversight agencies regarding real life service performance of over $2 billion in contracts. Leads multi-disciplinary, combined/joint teams addressing life, health, safety and infrastructure concerns in order to develop comprehensive Kandahar Airfield wide policies and procedures focused on improving installation readiness, base camp services and quality of life programs.

As noted above, upon completion of my Garrison Commander position, in Afghanistan, my Brigadier General, and commander of the 4th Expeditionary Sustainment Command (ESC), chose me, from all of his (full bird) Colonels, to replace him as the 4th ESC Rear Commander during his 1-year deployment to Kuwait. Ironically, Brigade Command was supposed to be a 2-year tour, but I spent the first year (of Brigade Command) deployed as a Garrison Commander and the second year (of Brigade Command) filling a 1-star General Officer (GO) position, and not just any GO position, but a "Commanding General" position. As the **Rear ESC Commander**, I commanded four Brigades (which included the Brigade that I was originally selected to command, along with three additional Brigades) and the ESC Staff consisting of 6,500 soldiers and civilians spread throughout 5 states (Texas, New Mexico, Oklahoma, Arkansas, and Louisiana). As a Colonel, I rated seven other Colonels (the four Brigade Commanders, and the ESC's Chief of Staff, G-3, Inspector General, and the ESC Internal Review Officers) and I senior rated 32 Lieutenant Colonels (LTCs), including 15 Battalion Commanders and 17 other staff LTCs.

I then PCS'd back to the Pentagon, for the third time, to serve as **Chief of Staff for the HQDA G-3/5/7 Force Management Directorate**. This position was short lived, as I was selected for promotion to Brigadier General within a few months of being assigned. I arrived at this position in April 2016, and was notified two months later, in June 2016 that I was selected for Brigadier General. I remained in this position for an additional eight months, in a promotable status, as a Colonel(P), before transitioning to my next job in February 2017.

In this job I was responsible for the management, coordination and execution of the internal operations of nine subordinate divisions, a Force Management School, and a

Force Management Support Agency, comprising over 250 personnel. I synchronized and integrated internal directorate operations in support of the Director, Deputy Director and subordinate divisions ensuring the accomplishment of organizational objectives. I managed directorate internal controls and business processes to enhance organizational efficiencies and effectiveness. I executed financial management and oversight for the directorate. Responsible for all aspects of personnel lifecycle management for the directorate. Coordinated organizational priorities in core mission areas with outside agencies to enhance directorate capabilities. And executed other priority missions as directed by the Director and Deputy Director.

Upon completing this third Pentagon assignment, I then pinned on the star, as a Brigadier General, and entered my new assignment as **Deputy Commanding General (DCG)** of the 80th Training Command in Richmond, VA. The Active Guard Reserve (AGR) program only goes up to Colonel (COL/O6), so when an AGR COL gets promoted to the General Officer rank, they must transition from the AGR to either the Troop Program Unit (TPU) program or the Individual Mobilization Augmentee (IMA) program. This

DCG position was a TPU billet, which means I was only required to work one weekend per month and two weeks of annual training. However, this shortened amount of days to work represents the minimum number of days you must do per year for a reservist to get credit for a "good year" of service. A TPU (or IMA) must have at least 20 "good years" of service to qualify for a reserve retirement at age 60. However, senior ranking officers (as a LTC serving in a key leadership position, or a COL, and definitely Generals) serve many more than the minimum days required. Since I transitioned from active duty status to part-time TPU status with over 25 years of active federal service (AFS), I was guaranteed an active duty retirement and not a reserve retirement, which means I began collecting my military retirement immediately upon retirement. Therefore, I chose not to work a civilian job upon my transition to TPU status, and instead to simply focus on working the maximum days allowed on TPU status and accepting all of the additional missions offered; and the General Officer Management Office (GOMO) will often request TPU and IMA Generals to volunteer to serve on additional assignments such as serving on promotion boards, serving as investigation officers (for 15-6 investigations when a COL or below needs to be investigated for misconduct), attending conferences where a USAR General must attend, training events where a USAR General is requested, etc. Needless to say, of the two years I served as a TPU General in the 80th Training Command, a total of one year's time (combined from all the separate duties) was spent on active duty. Therefore, I went into the job with nearly 25 ½ years of active federal status (AFS; or rather active duty credit towards an active retirement), and two years later I completed the job with 26 ½ years of AFS.

My duty description in this job read: Deputy Commanding General of 80th Training Command. Under the operational control (OPCON) of US Army Training and Doctrine Command (TRADOC), the 80th is a national-level Training Command with a global-support footprint. The command has an authorized strength of 7,360 soldiers and 322 civilians. The command structure contains 3 subordinate General Officer Division Headquarters, 11 School Brigades, 1 Training Support Brigade, 1 Multi-Functional Training Brigade, 63 Functional Battalions, 7 Training Centers, 4 Maintenance Sites, and 2 High-Tech Regional Training Sites. Units conduct military occupational specialty (MOS) Training for all service support and combat service support MOS's; the technical phases of the Noncommissioned Officer Education System (NCOES); Officer Intermediate Level Education (ILE); and Primary Developmental Education (PDE) instruction in both the Continental US (CONUS) and Outside the Continental US (OCONUS) locations. Responsible for all aspects of operations with emphasis on producing trained and ready soldiers capable of performing their wartime mission to standard.

In the General Officer ranks, although you can serve five years as a Brigadier General and five years as a Major General, you are not guaranteed that entire five years in each rank, you have to be "offered" a follow-on successive position. If you are not offered a follow-on position after your initial two- or three-year assignment is complete, you will then be separated from the military, or retired (if you have at least 20 years of creditable service). After I completed two years in the DCG position, I was fortunate enough to be offered a follow-on assignment as the **Mobilization Assistant to the Director of Strategic Planning** for U.S. Indo-Pacific Command (INDOPACOM), in Honolulu, HI. This was an Individual Mobilization Augmentee (IMA) position, which basically means I could serve a minimum of 70 days per year and a maximum of 365 depending on the amount the command could pay. During my 20 months in this position, I completed approximately 15 of those 20 months on active duty, bringing my total AFS to 28 years of AFS.

My duty description in this position was: To assist the Director in the Indo-Pacific Command's effort to shape and maintain regional security through development of diplomatic, economic, and military policies. This includes building and maintaining military-to-military and political-military relationships among the 36 nations within the Pacific region covering over 51% of the globe. Activities include disaster management, humanitarian assistance, homeland defense, appropriate oversight of reserve component matters, and, as a senior leader within the directorate, oversight of strategy and policy issues that influence the Pacific region.

Following this IMA position in Hawaii, at INDOPACOM, I was again fortunate to be offered a third General Officer position as the **Commander, U.S. Army Element and Deputy Director J3** of U.S. Africa Command (AFRICOM), in Stuttgart, Germany. This too was an IMA position. However, whereas the PACOM billet was IMA with the command paying to keep me on-orders for approximately 15 of the 20 months, AFRICOM paid to keep this billet occupied full-time with command sponsorship, which basically means I was full-time with my spouse's name on my orders for her to accompany me in Stuttgart. Although my spouse accompanying me was an added bonus, it was not the primary reason for command sponsorship. As the Deputy J3, I was required to be accessible 24-7 and I was required to occupy government quarters on post because the General Officer quarters on post have a secure communications suite in the basement that I needed 24-7 access to, consisting of secure/secret computers to work from home when required, and a Tandberg to conduct secure/secret level VTCs with the joint staff and sister Combatant Commands (COCOMs) during non-regular duty hours (which may be regular duty hours for those commands in different time zones), and the only way to occupy (GO-level) government quarters (on post) is to be command sponsored, because the government quarters are primarily for family members. Otherwise, if I did not require a secure communications suite in my home, I could have simply rented (or purchased) a home off post without being command sponsored, but then I would not have been able to fulfill my duties as the Deputy J3.

My duty description in this position was: Dual hatted as Commander of USAFRICOM's Army Element and Deputy Director to the J3 Director. As Commander, conducts non-judicial punishment proceedings for all Army personnel and serve as appellate authority under Article 15, Uniformed Code of Military Justice (UCMJ) to ensure the health, welfare, morale, and discipline of all Army personnel in the command. As J3 Deputy Director, provides oversight and direction to Current, Future, Counter-Terrorism, and Information Operations, Protection and Training, Exercise and Readiness Division Chiefs. Ensures constant coordination between the Joint Staff, other Geographic Combatant Commands, other Departments, Service and Functional commands, as well as established Combined/Joint Task Forces in order to meet national strategic objectives and enhance regional security, while operating in a COVID-19 environment.

MY BROTHERS & SISTERS

As I stated earlier, I am the youngest of eight. However, due to the large age differences we actually grew up in two different sets – there was the first set of five kids, then due to two or three miscarriages there was a five-year break in giving birth. Then, after five years, my parents had the second group of kids that I grew up in. Although both sets grew up in different locales, the first in the rural setting of Stafford County and the second only partially in Stafford but mostly in the urban city of Fredericksburg, we all experienced the same rough times and can tell an equally chilling childhood tale.

ALBERT (PETE) WASHINGTON: Pete, the oldest, born August 1955, enlisted in the Army right out of high school as a mechanic. He remained active for about seven years then joined the Army Reserve. He is married and has two grown children and four grandchildren. He lives in a community outside of Dallas, TX and (occasionally) drives a tractor trailer. He retired from the Army Reserve as both a soldier and a civil service Military Technician (Mil-Tech), which means he held a dual status with the government as a civil service (government civilian) mechanic during the week and as a member (soldier) of the Army Reserve when that same unit drilled on the weekends.

JOSEPH (JOE) WASHINGTON: Joe, the 2nd oldest, born July 1956, enlisted in the Air Force right out of high school as an air traffic controller for about seven years. During those seven years, he earned his Bachelor's degree in aeronautics and then left military service to manage an airport. He earned his Master's degree in public administration and worked for the Federal Aviation Administration (FAA) as a senior GS-15. He retired, with 35 plus years of federal service in 2022. He is married to a retired registered nurse, who ran a medical consulting business. They have two grown children and live in Fort Worth, TX. Their son is a lawyer and graduate of the University of Texas and their daughter is a schoolteacher and graduate of the University of North Texas.

CELIA (BABY-SIS) SWAIN: Baby-Sis, the 3rd oldest and oldest girl, born September 1957, enlisted in the Navy right out of high school as a Yeoman (administrative specialist). She took an 'early-out' after 15 years and now lives in Fredericksburg, VA. Her passion is sewing; she works part-time out of her home sewing quilts, clothing, etc. She has two grown children, one grandchild, and one great-grandchild. Her son, who is working on his Master's degree is a Chief Warrant Officer-4 (CWO4) in the Marines and her daughter spent four years in the Army, before returning to the Fredericksburg area.

AVIS BANKS: Avis, born February 1959, has consistently worked in hospital administration and other administrative jobs in Fredericksburg for the 40 plus years since she graduated from high school. She has two grown sons who live in the Fredericksburg area.

ALTHEA DOBBINS: Althea, born August 1960, enlisted in the Air Force right out of high school as a communications specialist. She served 11 years in the Air Force, then returned to the Fredericksburg area. She has one grown son, two grown daughters, and eight grandchildren. Her son, who graduated from North Carolina A&T, on an Air Force ROTC scholarship, was a Captain in the Air Force, as an Air Battle Manager (ABM) before exiting the military to reside in NC with his family. I had the honor of commissioning him at his graduation ceremony, during a two-week R&R leave from Iraq. He is also an Elder in the Mormon Church and working on his Doctorates in Business. One daughter owns a hair salon and the other daughter is also a college graduate.

CLAUDIA WASHINGTON: Claudia, born December 1965, lives in Fredericksburg and had four grown sons (one of whom who passed away) and four grandchildren. She raised all her children by herself just as our mother did. While one of her sons was tragically shot to death by someone who broke into his apartment to rob him, another son graduated from the University of Virginia with a Bachelor's degree in Spanish and Latin American Studies. Incidentally, during my college days, she and my sister Avis allowed me to grocery shop for free in their kitchens and take whatever I wanted from their fridge with no questions asked. Having all four of her children before age 20 and dropping out of high school because of it, she definitely started out in life with major obstacles to overcome. But in the Spring of 2007, at the age of 41, she graduated from Mary Washington University with a Bachelor's degree in Liberal Arts, with a concentration in African American Studies. In 2018, she earned an Associate degree of Registered Nursing, and is only one class short of a Master's degree, in Healthcare Management, from Mary Washington University.

FELICIA (LISH) WRIGHT: Lish, my youngest sister who is only two years older than me, born September 1968, and is married to a truck driver working for a sanitation collection company. Lish worked several jobs and then chose to be a stay-at-home mom after her last son was born. They have two grown daughters and two younger sons, and live in the Fredericksburg area. The oldest daughter works for the state government and owns her own small business with a patent making and selling ethnic headwraps (as she has a small passion for sewing). The second daughter graduated from George Mason University and works for the federal government. I am closer to this sister and the previous sister mentioned, Claudia, because we were the second group of three raised together. The first five siblings were almost all grown and out of the house while the latter three of us were growing up.

ADDITIONAL PICTURES

Part of Official 4-Person US Delegation to Niger, with US Ambassadors, to Attend their first-ever Freely Democratic Presidential Inauguration

Executive Leadership Course Certification in Singapore

Safari Adventure with Rhonda in South Africa

Cruise destinations to Port Limon (Left) and Antigua (Right)

Disney Resort in Hawaii (Left) and Santorini, Greece (Right)

SMALL QUIRKS ABOUT ME

- I enjoy exercising. On average, I've worked out approximately three times per week for as long as I can remember. My exercise workout consisted of 100 push-ups, 100 sit-ups, and running five miles. Now in my latter years, I still do it every other day (averaging three times per week), but I have switched from 100 sit-ups to 100 crunches, due to back pain from sit-ups, and switched from running five miles to alternating between walking for 90 minutes or bike-riding for 90 minutes to avoid the associated aches and pains that running causes on an aging body. I do not consider myself a stud, but I do put in the work to stay healthy and fit for someone in their 50s. A high metabolism is something I am only just beginning to fully appreciate now that I am getting older as I am finding—in my friends who have no regular exercise regimen—that staying in shape is much harder if you do not exercise regularly. Obviously, consistency is the key. I am six feet even and weigh approximately 195 lbs. with a 33-inch waist. Although I eat any and everything, that has been my height, weight, and measurement for as long as I can remember thanks to some solid genes and a little consistency with my routine. I would not consider myself a *gym-rat* because I can easily place other things above working out with no heartburn. I would however have to consider myself a *'PT stud,'* according to Army standards, because I have remarkably managed to max the Army Physical Fitness Test (APFT) with a score of 300 consistently since my commissioning in 1992 (obviously, I am dating myself here as the Army has since changed from a 300-point fitness test to another test). After I turned 45, I began falling below the maximum 300 amount (only very slightly) and scoring between 296-300, which is still exceedingly high compared to the average military person, at my age and rank, who would normally score in the low to mid 200s.

- I am a big movie buff. Before COVID, I often watched at least one new movie a week. I have absolutely no problem going to the movies by myself if my son or wife was not interested in going, a true sign of a *real* movie buff. Obviously, COVID changed our lives forever as I no longer find myself going to movies now that COVID restrictions have lightened.

- I love to play chess and sudoku. I play a few games each week (if not daily) either with a friend or on one of the interactive computer sites where you play other people live. I hate to brag, but I rarely lose (smile). I enjoy dominoes as well.

- I used to listen to Rush Limbaugh almost daily. I am neither a hard-line Conservative Republican nor a Liberal Democrat (I am actually a Moderate) but do enjoy talk-radio and news. Notice I said I "used to" listen to Rush almost daily. Several years before his death, I had to give him up as he became too much of an overbearing *blow hard* (as he is often called by the 'Left'), where I had to substitute him for the daily political news broadcast lineups that I watch regularly throughout the day. Do not misunderstand, I am a young (but maybe not so young anymore) black male so I still enjoy (old school) R&B, gospel, jazz, etc. I was a political science major so the entire political system interests me. Having grown up poor and still having many relatives who rely on the social service system, I can appreciate the Democratic viewpoint. However, now that I live a different lifestyle with a huge nest-egg of investments, I also appreciate the *'Capitalistic'* nature and viewpoint, the *'help those who help themselves'* attitude, and especially the tax advantages championed by the Republicans. For example, both my wife and I have always claimed zero deductions (to have the most taxes withheld) but instead of receiving a large refund, we still pay taxes every year. I have paid between $2-10K for the past 10 years because of the generous dividends, interest, and capital gains returns on all my investments. Is that fair (considering many of my other family/friends who do not even claim zero deductions receive a few thousand dollars back every year)? If you think that is a slight bit unfair, then you too may have more Republican traits than you realize. But, paying too much in taxes is actually a '*good*' problem to have because it means you have cash coming in, which is a problem many people would love to have. Still, I have far more Democratic viewpoints than Republican and although I have never voted for a Republican presidential candidate, I would still call myself a Moderate, because if the right Republican candidate came along, I would have no problem giving him or her my vote. I do try to listen to, read up on, and learn as much as I can about each candidate before casting my vote regardless of political party. My only Republican views center around money (i.e., the fiscal conservative decisions associated with taxes, tax cuts, tax rates, etc.) and I would also admit that I favor the more Republican viewpoints associated with security (i.e., immigration, civil liberties, interrogation techniques, etc.). However, most all my other viewpoints lean more Leftward – the reason I have yet to vote for a Republican, but that day is getting closer and closer.

- I enjoy talking about money (and making money grow) even more than politics. That speaks for itself considering the in-depth analogy I used with politics above (smile). This is however, something I try to work on because I fear money could very well be my demise. The bible says, "It is easier for a camel to fit through the eye of a needle than for a rich man to get into Heaven." Many people would call me a 'rich man' now and if I am not one now, I am definitely on my way to becoming one very soon. Ordinarily, that would be a good thing, considering where my *'starting line'* was in life, but from reading the bible verse quoted above, I am not quite sure how positive a Blessing my present and future wealth is.

- I hate the smell of smoke. The quickest way to make me leave a room is to light up a cigarette or cigar. I also dislike the smell of coffee, almost as much as the smell of smoke – but cigarette smoke is by far the worst for me. I am one of the few military members who do not like coffee.

- The highlight of my day was (in my earlier years) playing with my 'mini-me' and hearing what he learned each day. But obviously, as he has grown older and older, it is less and less "playing with him" and more a thing of simply enjoying to see him turn into a fine young man. It is also a great feeling to know that now that I am retired, he has taken over the *'family business,'* as he is not only a proud member of my same fraternity, Alpha Phi Alpha Fraternity, Inc, but he is also a military officer and in the same branch as me: Logistics.